Best Editorial Cartoons of the Year

BEST EDITORIAL CARTOONS OF THE YEAR

1982 EDITION

Edited by
CHARLES BROOKS

Foreword by MIKE PETERS

PELICAN PUBLISHING COMPANY
GRETNA 1982

Special acknowledgment is made to the following for permission to use copyrighted material in this volume:

Editorial cartoons by Gene Basset, © United Features Syndicate; Jim Berry, ©NEA; Douglas Borgstedt, © Editor and Publisher; Paul Conrad, © Los Angeles Times Syndicate; Bill De Ore, © Field Syndicate; Hugh Haynie, © Los Angeles Times Syndicate; Art Henrikson, ©Paddock Publications; Frank Interlandi, © Los Angeles Times Syndicate; Dick Locher, © Chicago Tribune—New York News Syndicate; Michael Konopacki, © Rothco and IUE News; Al Liederman, © Rothco; Jimmy Margulies, © Rothco; David Wiley Miller, ©Copley News Service; John Milt Morris, © The Associated Press; Bill Garner, © United Features Syndicate; Mike Peters, © United Features Syndicate; Don Wright, ©New York Times Syndicate; Lee Judge, © Field Syndicate; John Trever, © Field Syndicate.

Library of Congress Serial Catalog Data

Best editorial cartoons. 1972-
    Gretna [La.] Pelican Pub. Co.
    v. 29cm. annual-
"A pictorial history of the year."

    I. United States- Politics and government—
1969—Caricatures and Cartoons—Periodicals.
E839.5.B45   320.9'7309240207   73-643645
ISSN 0091-2220   MARC-S

Manufactured in the United States of America

Published by Pelican Publishing Company, Inc.
1101 Monroe St., Gretna, Louisiana 70053

Designed by Barney McKee

Contents

Foreword

My cartoon ideas usually focus on a subject for which I have a great deal of concern. I believe this is of critical importance in creating a successful editorial cartoon. If I do not care about the issue involved, then my readers are not going to care. I do a lot of cartoons about the Equal Rights Amendment, a topic that I care about desperately. Yet there may be only one out of five cartoons that I do on this subject that people will react to. I have to really feel a subject in my gut before I can communicate it effectively to people. I get no vibes, for example, about President Reagan or the Gross National Product. On the other hand, I feel deeply about poor people not eating or not having jobs, and this, I think, is reflected in much of my work.

You will see many cartoons similar to this: a big truck, labeled "The Economy," with President Reagan in the front throwing a monkey wrench into the motor. That topic does not appeal to me at all, so I do not try to get that message across in my cartoons.

Once I decide to draw about a particular issue, I generally know what I am going to say. The ERA is a good example. I know that I want to say that the ERA is in trouble and that women are still downtrodden. It is no longer popular to be a proponent of ERA because most people are convinced that it has lost its momentum. In my opinion, women are still second-class citizens, just as they were before the 1970s.

As I begin to work, I sometimes find myself staring at a blank piece of paper, hoping that the angel of inspiration will come down, tap me on the shoulder, and say: "Here's your idea for the day, Mike." Many people have this misconception about cartoonists. They seem to think we wake up in the middle of the night, come up with ideas inspired from on high, and then go to the office and knock out something in a few minutes. That has never happened to me. I have never received inspiration in the middle of the night for a cartoon.

A cartoonist friend of mine decided it would be fun to devise a stock way of originating cartoon ideas. He thought it would be amusing to tell people that he had two shoe boxes. One was labeled the topic box, containing different subjects selected from the daily news such as ERA, or President Reagan and the economy, or Nancy Reagan's china. The other box was reserved for approaches to cartoons (general, hackneyed ideas that we editorial cartoonists use to put across ideas: a man on a deserted island, or a Shakespearean phrase, or a nursery rhyme, or a Benjamin Franklin quote such as "A penny saved is a penny earned").

The procedure was to shut your eyes, stick your hand in the topic box, and pick out a piece of paper. It might say "Reagan and the Economy." Then, you reached into the approach box and pulled out a slip that might say "Alice in Wonderland." Finally, you combined the approach and the topic to get the day's cartoon. Well, it never worked for either of us. We chose the North Atlantic Treaty Alliance disarmament as the topic and Winnie the Pooh as the approach. The idea, of course, was an absolute failure. What at first sounded like a good, easy formula could never work.

Routinely, I arrive at the office around 6:30 or seven o'clock in the morning. I usually allow for about an hour and a half to work on the previous day's cartoon, which must be finished by my nine o'clock deadline. I will have jotted down a number of topics the night before after reading several newspapers and watching the television news. I drive my wife and children crazy switching channels back and forth, but it is an effective method for me.

As I begin the new cartoon for the day, I sit and stare at a blank piece of drawing paper. Sometimes the staring lasts for hours. What a matchless torment it is to still have a blank sheet of paper at four o'clock in the afternoon. That can be demoralizing, so I try to start fairly early to ensure that it does not happen.

Having selected two likely topics, I then begin to brainstorm. Brainstorming can work great in a group, but it is not easy to do by oneself. By definition, brainstorming is an exchange of ideas between two or more people, so one person can be approximately one too few. Nevertheless, I have managed to create my own particular method of brainstorming.

I sit at the drawing board and experiment with my idea. Let's say I want to do something on the ERA. I know, generally, what I want to say about the ERA, but I will search for a new approach. Given the fact that I have drawn a thousand cartoons on the subject of the ERA, I have to find the 1001st idea. I might picture a wheel with about ten or fifteen spokes, radiating outward from the ERA in the center. I then try to write something that represents women on each spoke. I might jot down Adam and Eve, Whistler's Mother, the Susan B. Anthony dollar, the Mona Lisa, Little Miss Muffet, or the Old Lady in the Shoe. Then I attempt to connect them, or determine which visualization might be a new and effective way to convey the message. Primarily, this process helps me overcome my fear of the blank sheet of paper, and it helps me *not to accept the first idea* that occurs to me.

When I first began drawing cartoons, and for many years afterward, one of my biggest problems was drawing the first idea that came into my mind, instead of going for the second, or third, or fiftieth idea. I have found that the first idea usually is the most obvious. It is the one that fifty other cartoonists will be doing the same day. That is one of the reasons why brainstorming with myself is so beneficial. It provides me with about four or five other ideas that I might not have thought of had I settled for the first knee-jerk idea. Furthermore, it gives me a couple of extra ways to put across an idea the next time I want to deal with that subject.

This idea of brainstorming is certainly not new. In fact, cartoonists such as George Booth, Sam Gross, Charles Adams, and Charles Rodriguez have been doing something called single-theme spread, which is similar to single brainstorming. The single-theme approach can be used when the drawing of cartoons is confined exclusively to one topic. Sam Gross is a master of this technique.

Picture, for example, the gingerbread man running down a path in the forest. With a little imagination, he can become a jogger, or perhaps he is chased by a dog. The method is to extrapolate ideas from the theme and to keep making those ideas more and more bizarre. The cartoonist tries to create the most ridiculous situation imaginable.

There is, of course, no stock way of developing ideas for cartoons. Ideas are a nebulous, natural phenomenon that one can never quite master. Good ideas are born from blood, sweat, tears, and I often have concluded that providence had a great deal to do with their creation—in my case, anyway.

MIKE PETERS
Editorial Cartoonist
Dayton Daily News

Award-Winning Cartoons

1981 PULITZER PRIZE

MIKE PETERS
Editorial Cartoonist
Dayton Daily News

Born October 9, 1943, in St. Louis, Missouri; earned bachelor's degree in fine arts from Washington University, 1965; joined staff of *Chicago Daily News* as cartoonist in 1965; served as U. S. Army artist in Okinawa, 1966-1967; rejoined staff of *Chicago Daily News*; editorial cartoonist for the *Dayton* (Ohio) *Daily News*, 1969 to present; cartoons syndicated through United Features Syndicate; author of three books; cartoonist in residence for NBC's "Today" show; his work also appears on NBC's Nightly News; winner of Sigma Delta Chi Award for cartooning, 1975; Overseas Press Award, 1976; and Distinguished Alumni Award from Washington University, 1981.

1981 NATIONAL HEADLINERS CLUB AWARD

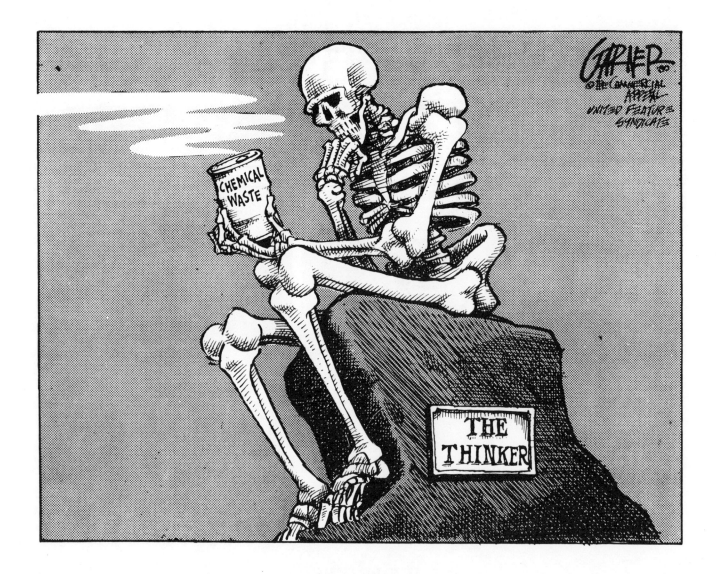

BILL GARNER
Editorial Cartoonist
Memphis Commercial Appeal

A native Texan; served for three years as cartoonist and illustrator for the *Pacific Stars and Stripes* in Tokyo; staff artist and editorial cartoonist for the Washington *Star*, 1963-1976; editorial cartoonist for the Memphis *Commercial Appeal*, 1976 to present; paints in acrylics and watercolors; has had portraits and landscapes exhibited in various galleries.

1980 SIGMA DELTA CHI AWARD
(Selected in 1981)

U.S. DECLARES VICTORY IN WAR ON POVERTY AND PULLS OUT. – NEWS ITEM

PAUL CONRAD
Editorial Cartoonist
Los Angeles Times

1981 OVERSEAS PRESS CLUB AWARD

HARA-CARI

PAUL CONRAD
Editorial Cartoonist
Los Angeles Times

Began career as student cartoonist for the *Daily Iowan* at the University of Iowa; editorial cartoonist for the *Denver Post* for fourteen years; chief editorial cartoonist for the *Los Angeles Times* since 1964; winner of Pulitzer Prize for editorial cartooning, 1964 and 1971; winner of three awards for excellence from Sigma Delta Chi and one from the Overseas Press Club; cartoons distributed by the Los Angeles Times Syndicate.

1980 NATIONAL
NEWSPAPER AWARD/CANADA
(Selected in 1981)

THE NEW FATHERS OF CONFEDERATION

VIC ROSCHKOV
Editorial Cartoonist
Toronto Star

Born in Kiev, the Ukraine, 1942; with his family, left a displaced persons camp in Belgium in 1950 and moved to Canada; lived in Montreal, North Bay, Windsor, London, and Brantford, where he worked as dishwasher, tobacco-picker, and cement factory laborer; became interested in drawing caricatures, selling one to the Canadian edition of *Time* magazine; later joined *Windsor Star* as full-time political cartoonist; editorial cartoonist for *Toronto Star*, 1976-1981; left the *Star* to form his own cartoon syndicate.

Best Editorial Cartoons of the Year

MIKE GRASTON
Courtesy Windsor Star (Ont.)

The Reagan Administration

"Reaganomics," President Reagan's economic plan to stimulate investment and work effort, was unveiled during the year. According to the plan, an oppressive federal income tax system was responsible for undermining economic growth. The major premise of Reaganomics is that by cutting taxes and allowing business and workers to keep more of their earnings, additional capital will be available for expansion and modernization—thus creating more jobs. And, furthermore, if workers are allowed to keep more of their paychecks, there will be more inclination to save and perhaps even to invest in business.

Since assuming office, President Reagan has moved swiftly toward so-called "supply-side economics." Many marginal welfare programs have been curtailed and taxes have been reduced. At year's end he asked for time to give the program a chance to work.

The Reagan Administration continued to talk tough to the Soviets, declaring repeatedly that *detente* is a two-way street. In a turnabout of President Carter's policy, Reagan eased official U.S. criticism of South Africa's racial policies. He also continued to demand the removal of Cuban troops from Angola and Soviet forces from Afghanistan.

DICK WRIGHT
Courtesy Providence (R.I.)
Journal–Bulletin

HUGH HAYNIE
Courtesy Louisville Courier–Journal

DICK LOCHER
Courtesy Chicago Tribune

JIM BORGMAN
Courtesy Cincinnati Enquirer

"CONGRATULATIONS, STOCKMAN... WE FINALLY GOT THE FEDERAL GOVERNMENT DOWN TO THE SIZE WE WANTED!"

CHUCK BROOKS
Courtesy Birmingham News

MIKE PETERS
Courtesy Dayton Daily News

GIVE ME YOUR *TRULY* TIRED, YOUR *TRULY* POOR, YOUR *TRULY* HUDDLED MASSES...

GENE BASSET
© United Features Syndicate

FRANK INTERLANDI
Courtesy Los Angeles Times

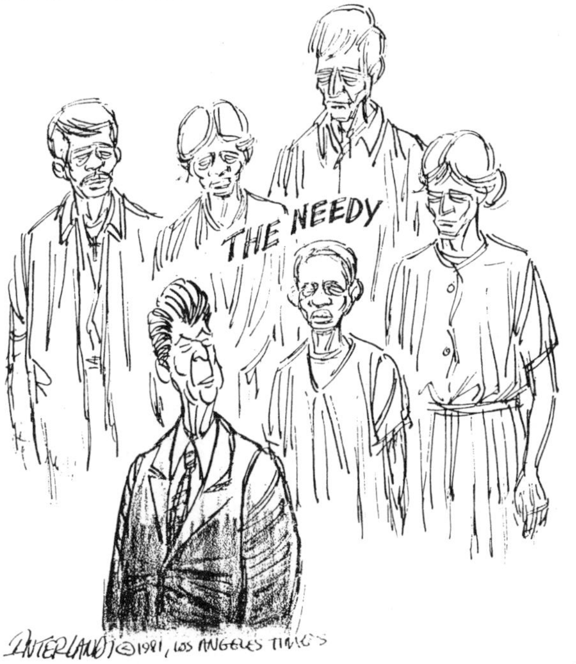
THE NEEDY
INTERLANDI ©1981, LOS ANGELES TIMES

"AS WE SAY IN SHOW BIZ, DON'T CALL US, WE'LL CALL YOU!"

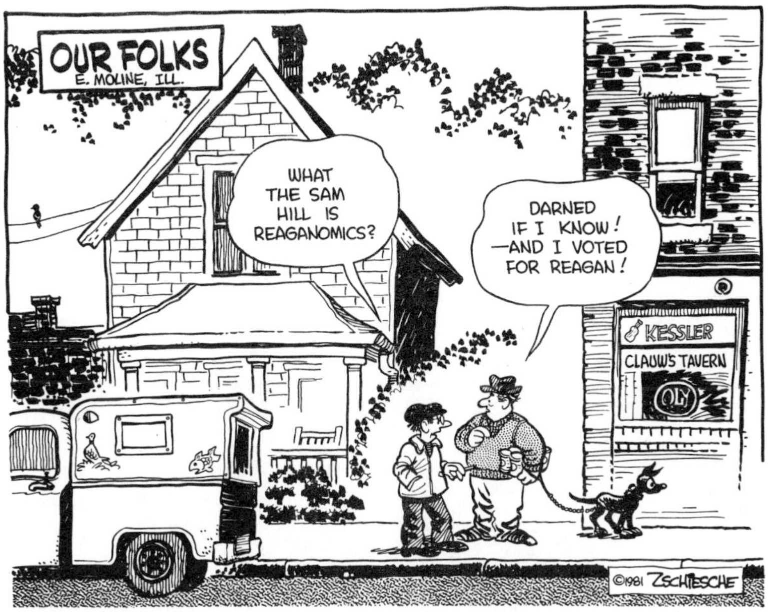
OUR FOLKS
E. MOLINE, ILL.
WHAT THE SAM HILL IS REAGANOMICS?
DARNED IF I KNOW! —AND I VOTED FOR REAGAN!
KESSLER
CLAUW'S TAVERN
©1981 ZSCHIESCHE

BOB ZSCHIESCHE
Courtesy Our Folks

ED GAMBLE
Courtesy Florida Times–Union

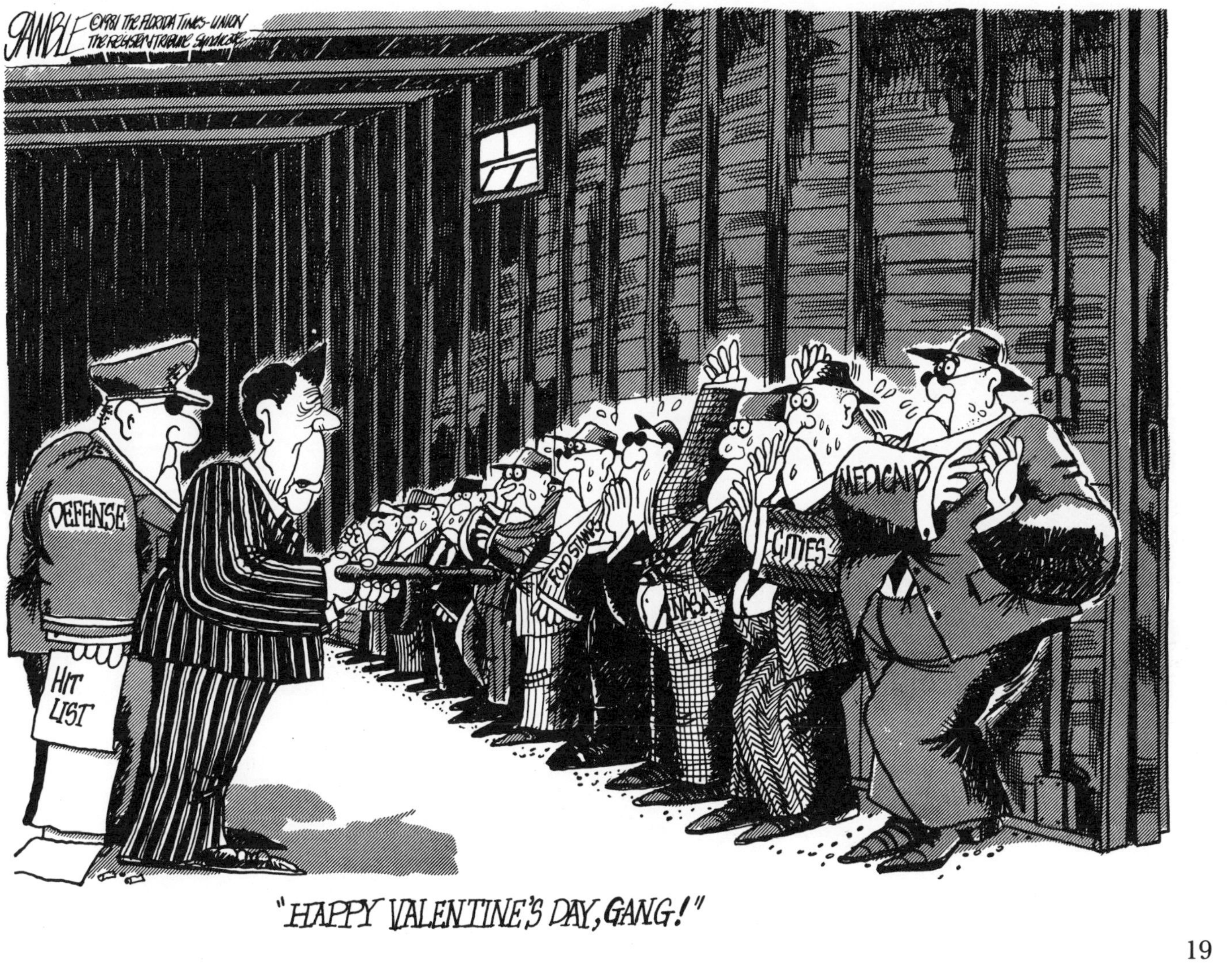
GAMBLE ©1981 THE FLORIDA TIMES-UNION THE REGISTER TRIBUNE SYNDICATE
DEFENSE
HIT LIST
FOOD STAMPS
NASA
CITIES
MEDICAID

"HAPPY VALENTINE'S DAY, GANG!"

CORKY
Courtesy Honolulu Star–Bulletin

PHIL BISSELL
Courtesy Lowell (Mass.) Sun

JIM BERRY
©NEA

ELDON PLETCHER
Courtesy New Orleans Times–Picayune

"I can't come out and play now. I've got to work for a couple of hours."

JOHN TREVER
Courtesy Albuquerque Journal

DOUG MACGREGOR
Courtesy Norwich Bulletin

GENE BASSET
© United Features Syndicate

"These Are For Every Day....What Do We Have For Halloween?"

CHARLES BISSELL
Courtesy The Tennessean

H. CLAY BENNETT
Courtesy St. Petersburg Times

JOHN CRAWFORD
Courtesy Alabama Journal

"NOT TO WORRY, MR. PRESIDENT... JUST AN IMPATIENT CITIZEN FROM FLEA HOP, ALABAMA WANTING TO KNOW IF YOU'VE HAD TIME YET TO WHIP INFLATION."

KEVIN KALLAUGHER
Courtesy Sunday Journal (Eng.)

"Did somebody want me?"

OUR AIM IS RIGHT ABOUT HERE!

ROY CARLESS
Courtesy Steel Labor, VE News

HEAD START

23

FEARLESS FOSDICK

BLAINE
Courtesy The Spectator (Ont.)

SAM RAWLS
Courtesy Atlanta Journal

PAT CROWLEY
Courtesy The Post (W. Palm Beach)

"Our long national nightmare is over."

BRIAN GABLE
Courtesy Regina Leader–Post (Sask.)

GEORGE FISHER
Courtesy Arkansas Gazette

ED ASHLEY
Courtesy Toledo Blade

MIKE JENKINS
Courtesy Beaumont Enterprise

PAUL DUGINSKI
Courtesy Sacramento Union

LARRY WRIGHT
Courtesy Detroit News

DRAPER HILL
Courtesy Detroit News

TOM MEYER
Courtesy San Francisco Chronicle

O'Neill
and the Democrats

After Ronald Reagan was swept into the presidency and the Republicans gained control of the Senate in the 1980 elections, the job of speaker of the House of Representatives became a particularly important post for the Democrats. Thomas P. "Tip" O'Neill, a Democrat from Massachusetts, occupied that position and led liberal opposition to the new wave of conservatism.

Republican lawmakers were joined by conservative Democrats in a broad effort to reduce federal spending programs. Reagan won smashing victories on his proposed budget and on tax cuts, in spite of strenuous opposition by O'Neill and his followers.

In October, O'Neill battled the president again on the sale of five Airborne Warning and Control System (AWACS) airplanes to Saudi Arabia. Just when it appeared O'Neill and the Democrats had blocked the sale, Reagan picked up a few critical votes and triumphed again.

President Carter had suffered such a crushing defeat in the 1980 campaign that he decided to stay out of Washington politics. The mantle of Democratic leadership fell to O'Neill, who emerged repeatedly from the fray with nose bloodied.

RAY OSRIN
Courtesy Cleveland Plain Dealer

THE COMPROMISE.

JIM MAZZOTTA
Ft. Myers News–Press

'Yipe, Yipe, Yipe. . . .'

EDDIE GERMANO
Courtesy Brockton Daily Enterprise

EUGENE CRAIG
Courtesy Columbus Dispatch

BRUCE PLANTE
Courtesy Fayetteville Times (N.C.)

JIM BORGMAN
Courtesy Cincinnati Enquirer

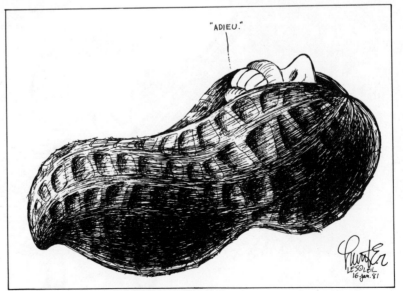

RAOUL HUNTER
Courtesy Le Soleil (Que.)

JIM LANGE
Courtesy Daily Oklahoman

SANDY CAMPBELL
Courtesy The Tennessean

DICK LOCHER
Courtesy Chicago Tribune

STILL TRYIN' TO FIGURE IT OUT

VERN THOMPSON
Courtesy Lawton (Okla.) Constitution

DICK LOCHER
Courtesy Chicago Tribune

Congress

Congress took a close look at the election mandate of 1980, and in 1981 helped President Reagan begin to turn around federal economic policy. It was the most abrupt change in direction for America's government since Franklin D. Roosevelt's New Deal.

The proposed AWACS (Airborne Warning and Control System) aircraft sale to Saudi Arabia was the most controversial foreign-policy issue Congress had to face. Almost until the moment of the vote, observers had predicted the president would suffer his first major policy defeat, but once again Reagan surprised the experts and emerged the winner.

Congress cut almost $34.2 billion from the fiscal 1982 budget originally proposed by President Carter, tracking almost precisely the budget proposed by Reagan. Congress also approved a tax-reduction bill that included a 25-percent cut in individual tax rates over three years and a significant provision known as indexing. Beginning in 1985, income tax rates will be indexed to offset the effects of inflation.

Congressmen also sweetened their own finances during the year. They voted themselves income-tax exemptions if they owned homes both in the District of Columbia and at home. They also lifted the lid on honorariums for members of Congress.

ED GAMBLE
Courtesy Florida Times–Union

JERRY FEARING
Courtesy St. Paul Dispatch–
Pioneer Press

KEN ALEXANDER
Courtesy San Francisco Examiner

TIMOTHY ATSEFF
Courtesy Syracuse Herald-Journal

KARL HUBENTHAL
Courtesy Los Angeles Herald–Examiner

BERT WHITMAN
Courtesy Phoenix Gazette

ED STEIN
Courtesy Rocky Mountain News

JACK MCLEOD
Courtesy Buffalo Evening News

EUGENE PAYNE
Courtesy Charlotte Observer

DON WRIGHT
Courtesy Miami News

MIKE MORGAN
Courtesy Macon Telegraph & News

ROBERT RICH
Courtesy Knoxville News–Sentinel

JIM PALMER
Courtesy Montgomery Advertiser

DRAPER HILL
Courtesy Detroit News

WAYNE STAYSKAL
Courtesy Chicago Tribune

"HOW DO I KNOW THIS IS A GOOD HONEST BRIBE AND NOT ONE OF THOSE UNDERHANDED ABSCAM THINGS?"

National Defense

National defense received much higher priority in President Reagan's administration than had been the case under President Carter. In October, after nine months of intensive study, Reagan announced a plan for modernizing U.S. strategic forces. He proposed $180.3 billion to bring land, sea, and air defense up to the desired levels.

The Reagan White House rejected Carter's plan for mobile MX missiles, planning instead for the deployment of a limited number of MX missiles in superhardened silos built to withstand a nuclear blast. Reagan also revived the B-1 bomber and asked for continued research on the "Stealth" bomber, as well as a more powerful and more accurate missile for U. S. Trident nuclear submarines.

In August, Reagan ordered the unilateral production of neutron weapons, which are lethal to humans but do less damage to property than conventional nuclear arms. The move was primarily intended as a deterrent to a Russian tank invasion of Western Europe. In response to a reporter's question, Reagan noted that in case a nuclear war broke out in Europe, the conflict could be confined to that area. Peace demonstrators in Europe interpreted his remark as a plan to make Eastern Europe an atomic battlefield, ignoring the missiles' intended purpose as a last-line defense for Europe.

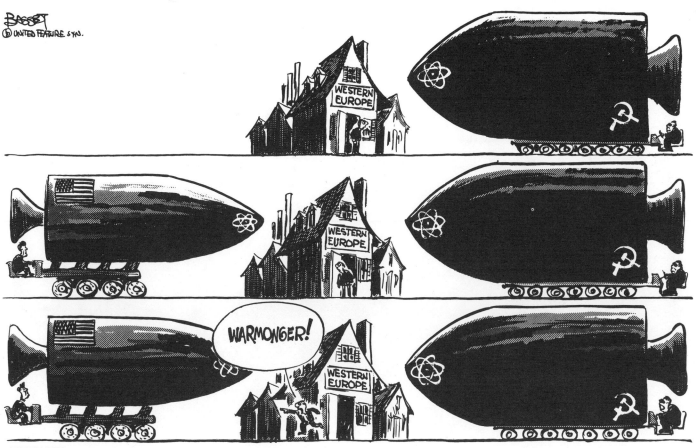

GENE BASSET
© United Features Syndicate

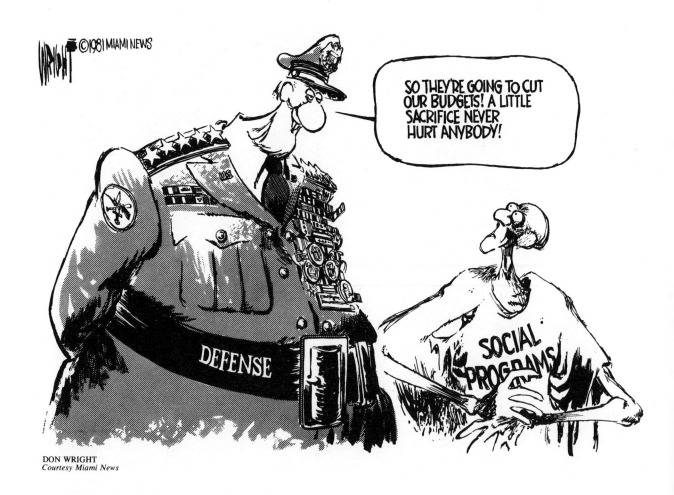

DON WRIGHT
Courtesy Miami News

DAVID HORSEY
Courtesy Seattle Post–Intelligencer

JERRY DOYLE
Courtesy Philadelphia Daily News

PAUL CONRAD
Courtesy Los Angeles Times

'WINDOW OF VULNERABILITY'

BILL SANDERS
Courtesy Milwaukee Journal

TOM MEYER
Courtesy San Francisco Chronicle

SAM RAWLS
Courtesy Atlanta Journal

DICK WALLMEYER
*Courtesy Independent Press–Telegram
(Calif.)*

BILL SANDERS
Courtesy Milwaukee Journal

EDD ULUSCHAK
Courtesy Edmonton Journal

"Those were highlights of President Reagan's latest hard-line speech — now the weather. Record highs of plus 8,000 degrees were set in some parts of . . ."

BRIAN GABLE
Courtesy Regina Leader–Post (Sask.)

ROGER HARVELL
Courtesy Pine Bluff Commercial

JIMMY JOHNSON
Courtesy Jackson (Miss.) Daily News

AL LIEDERMAN
© Rothco

FRANK EVERS
Courtesy New York Daily News

JACK MCLEOD
Courtesy Buffalo Evening News

CHARLES DANIEL
Courtesy Knoxville Journal

TIM MENEES
Courtesy Pittsburgh Post–Gazette

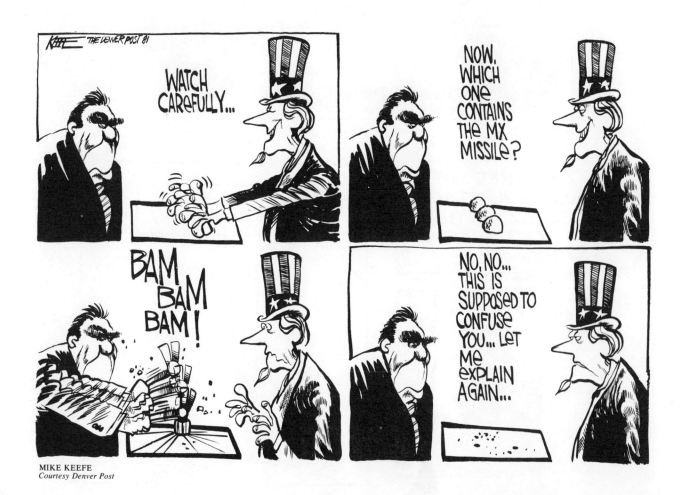

MIKE KEEFE
Courtesy Denver Post

THE HUMAN RACE

LOU GRANT
Courtesy Oakland Tribune

"IT'S THE NICE MAN FROM THE JOINT CHIEFS, HARVEY — HERE TO SEE ABOUT THE MX BASING MODE AGAIN!"

JOHN TREVER
Courtesy Albuquerque Journal

"WELL, THANK GOD, WITH THE GOING MORTGAGE RATES, THE NEUTRON BOMB LEFT OUR HOME INTACT!"

MERLE TINGLEY
Courtesy London Free Press (Can.)

WE GOT YOUR DEPLOYMENT PROBLEM LICKED, MR. PRESIDENT! WAIT'LL YOU SEE IT! IT'LL DRIVE THEM ROOSKIES OUTA THEIR GOURDS

GEORGE FISHER
Courtesy Arkansas Gazette

JOHN BRANCH
Courtesy San Antonio Express-News

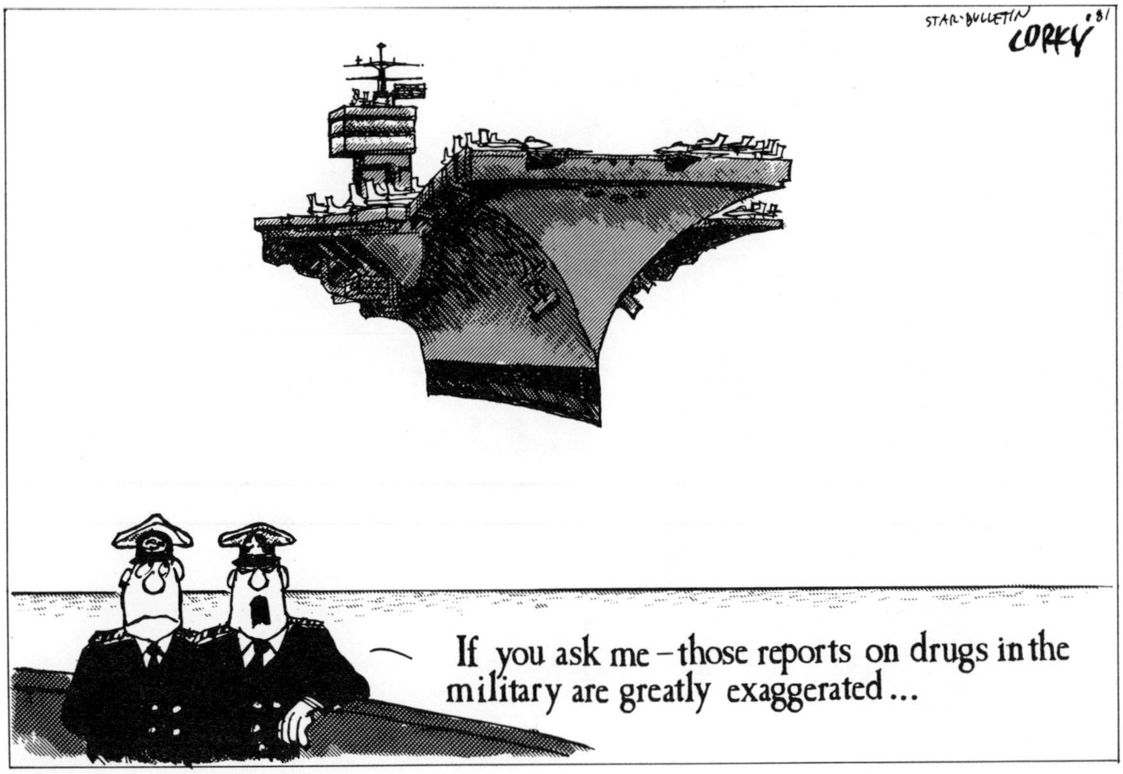
STAR-BULLETIN
CORKY '81
If you ask me – those reports on drugs in the military are greatly exaggerated...

CORKY
Courtesy Honolulu Star–Bulletin

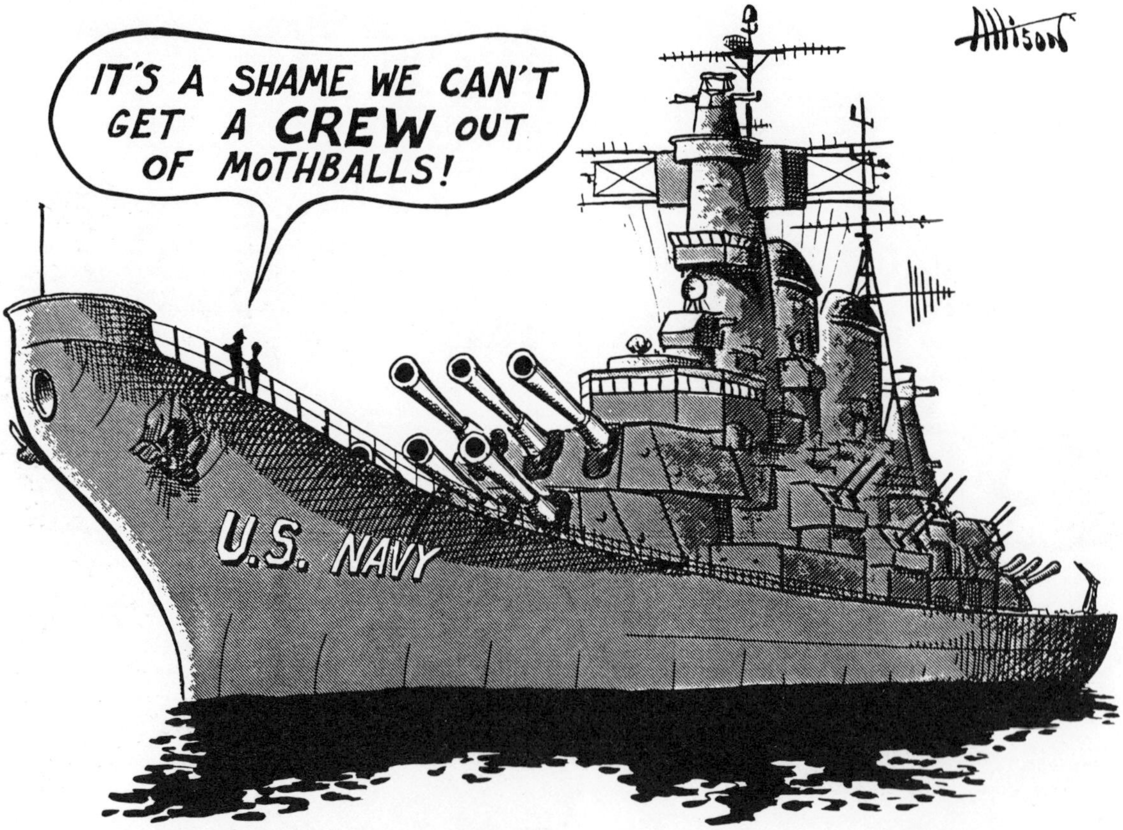
ALLISON
IT'S A SHAME WE CAN'T GET A CREW OUT OF MOTHBALLS!
U.S. NAVY

RICHARD ALLISON
Courtesy Army Times

The Economy

"Sluggish" was the most accurate term to describe the U.S. economy throughout 1981, with inflation having soared to 12.4 percent in 1980 and the unemployment rate having risen to 7.4 percent. President Reagan's first task in office was to address economic conditions. The productivity of American workers was declining, and the automobile and housing industries were practically in a depression.

The year 1981 began with the prime rate at 21.5 percent and remained high all year, seemingly immune to President Reagan's cut in federal spending. Inflation, however, was trimmed significantly, hovering between 8 and 9 percent for much of the year.

A surplus of oil on the world market kept oil prices depressed, but the automobile industry continued in the doldrums for the third straight year. Foreign auto makers took over a record 26.5 percent of the market. The steel industry continued to suffer as foreign imports took their toll.

Business failures in the first 10 months of the year were well ahead of the totals for the recession years of 1975 and 1980 and the highest since 1962. Some 750 automobile dealerships were forced to close in 1981, and bankruptcies among construction firms increased by 50 percent.

"...I'LL ADMIT IT'S NOT WHAT YOU EXPECTED BUT IT'S ONLY GONNA BE A SHORT RIDE!"

CLIFF BALDOWSKI
Courtesy Atlanta Constitution

JIM LARRICK
Courtesy Clarion–Ledger (Miss.)

ART HENRIKSON
ⓒPaddock Publications

HOW DEAD IS HE, DOC?

FRANK EVERS
Courtesy New York Daily News

STOCK EXCHANGE

EXPRESS WINDOW
8 SHARES OR LESS

ADRIAN RAESIDE
Courtesy Times–Colonist (B.C.)

LEE JUDGE
Courtesy Kansas City Times

E.F. HUTTON

WHEN RONALD REAGAN TALKS...

DARCY   Newsday cartoon by Tom Darcy

THE ECONOMY

'The question is not whether we like what is happening to
Dr. Jekyll, but whether Mr. Hyde will invest his savings!'

TOM DARCY
Courtesy Newsday

TOM CURTIS
Courtesy Milwaukee Sentinel

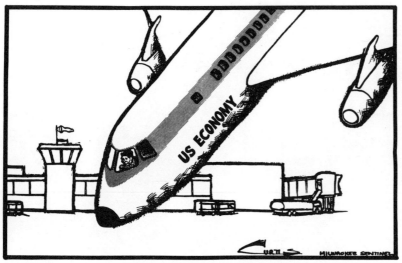

"We cannot delay . . ." —Reagan

H. CLAY BENNETT
Courtesy St. Petersburg Times

JOHN BRANCH
Courtesy San Antonio Express–News

Foreign Affairs

Secretary of State Alexander Haig stumbled into the center of controversy several times during the course of the year. After President Reagan was shot on March 30, Haig nervously told a group of reporters in the White House "I am in control here." His remarks were beamed to a huge television audience. Haig had mistakenly assumed he was third in the line of succession to power after the president and vice-president. In reality, he was fifth.

Haig's critics, of whom there are many, cited this as one more example of his over-assertiveness. His supporters maintained he had been correct in stressing to the world that the government was operating smoothly at a perilous time.

When El Salvador's government was threatened by guerrillas, Reagan asked Congress for increased military and economic aid. Military advisers were authorized, but vocal critics contended aid to El Salvador would lead to "another Vietnam."

The Soviets had their troubles as well. On October 27, a Russian submarine ran aground only nine miles from the Swedish coast. High radiation levels were found aboard the sub, leading to speculation it was carrying nuclear weapons. After a tense several days, Swedish authorities released the craft.

JON KENNEDY
Courtesy Arkansas Democrat

The Shopkeeper

WHO SAYS WE DON'T HAVE A FOREIGN POLICY?

JOHN MILT MORRIS
©The Associated Press

DWANE POWELL
Courtesy News & Observer (N.C.)

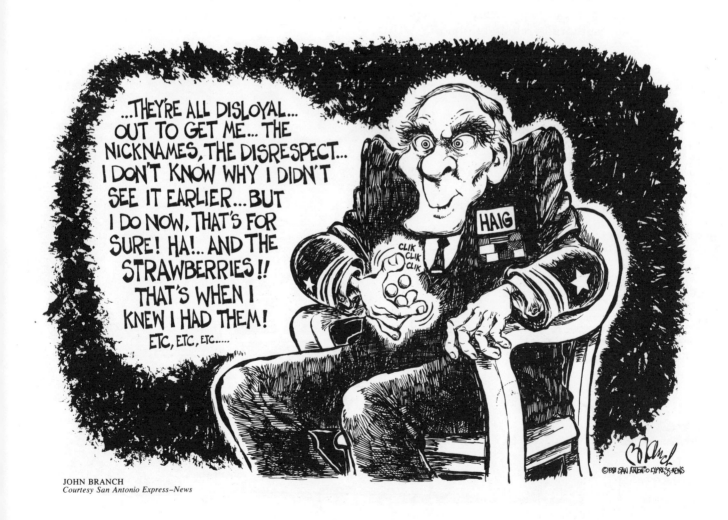

JOHN BRANCH
Courtesy San Antonio Express–News

54

BLAINE
Courtesy The Spectator (Ont.)

GENE BASSET
© United Features Syndicate

BILL GARNER
Courtesy Commercial Appeal (Memphis)

". . .CRISIS CHIEF REPORTING AS ORDERED, SIR!"

CLIFF BALDOWSKI
Courtesy Atlanta Constitution

DOUG MACGREGOR
Courtesy Norwich Bulletin

CHESTER COMMODORE
Courtesy Chicago Defender

DENNIS RENAULT
Courtesy Sacramento Bee

'If our Military advisors aren't successful, we'll bomb Hanoi and mine Haiphong. Then we'll defoliate Danang and Hue and setup strategic hamlets here, around Saigon!'

BOB TAYLOR
Courtesy Dallas Times–Herald

"THOSE WHO CANNOT REMEMBER THE PAST,
ARE CONDEMNED TO REPEAT IT"

TOM CURTIS
Courtesy Milwaukee Sentinel

"This time, let's call this one Nicaragua, this one El Salvador, this one Honduras . . ."

CLYDE PETERSON
Courtesy Houston Chronicle

'That's the trouble with rookies — you don't know if he's wild
or if that's exactly where he was aiming'

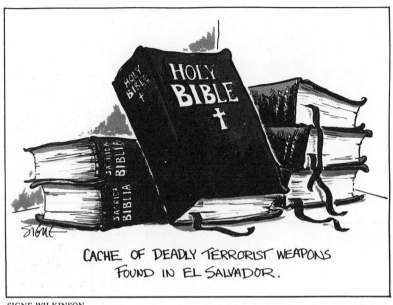

CACHE OF DEADLY TERRORIST WEAPONS FOUND IN EL SALVADOR.

SIGNE WILKINSON
Courtesy Philadelphia Inquirer

El Salvador's ruling junta gives opponents a little push!

LUIS BORJA
Courtesy Caricatura Nacional

DAVID WILEY MILLER
©Copley News Service

EDD ULUSCHAK
Courtesy Edmonton Journal

"What do you mean you've lost the urge to kill — what kind of Christian *are* you?"

TERRY MOSHER (AISLIN)
Courtesy Montreal Gazette

DICK WRIGHT
*Courtesy Providence (R.I.)
Journal–Bulletin*

"...DON'T FORGET TO TELL YOUR FRIENDS ABOUT US!!.."

"CAN I HELP YOU?"

PAT CROWLEY
Courtesy The Post (W. Palm Beach)

IF I WEREN'T AN INTELLECTUAL AND DIDN'T KNOW BETTER, I'D **SWEAR** THOSE WERE RUSSIAN TANKS AND MISSILES.

JIM BERRY
©NEA

"I liked the arms race much better when we were the only ones in it!"

RICHARD ALLISON
Courtesy Army Times

JACK JURDEN
*Courtesy Wilmington Evening
Journal–News*

TOM ENGELHARDT
Courtesy St. Louis Post–Dispatch

CHUCK AYERS
Courtesy Akron Beacon–Journal

64

PAUL SZEP
Courtesy Boston Globe

BREZHNEV WARNS US ON ARMS RACE

ED GAMBLE
Courtesy Florida Times–Union

EUGENE PAYNE
Courtesy Charlotte Observer

DRUG TRAFFIC STRANGLING
LATIN AMERICA

ANGEL ZAMARRIPAL
Mexico

"ENGLAND"

CARLOS B. MALVIDO
Mexico

KIRK WALTERS
Courtesy Patuxent Publishing Corp.

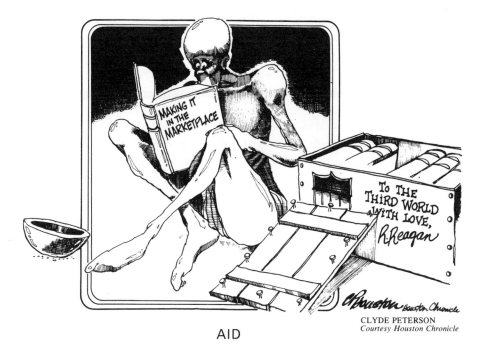

AID

CLYDE PETERSON
Courtesy Houston Chronicle

SCOTT WILLIS
Courtesy Cleveland Press

67

Guns and Assassins

Assassins gunned down three world leaders during 1981—President Reagan, Pope John Paul II, and Egypt's Anwar Sadat. Reagan and the Pope survived, but Sadat was killed.

John Hinckley Jr., a young drifter, allegedly pumped six shots at the president from short range as Reagan was leaving a Washington, D.C., hotel on March 30. The president was struck in the left side, and three others were wounded, including White House Press Secretary James Brady. Although in serious condition when he arrived at the George Washington University hospital, Reagan staged a miraculous recovery and within weeks resumed a full work schedule.

On May 13 Pope John Paul II was wounded by an escaped Turkish terrorist in St. Peter's Square in Rome. It was not until August 14 that the pontiff was finally discharged from the hospital for the last time. The assailant was convicted of attempted murder and sentenced to life in prison.

Sadat was assassinated in Cairo on October 6 as he watched a military parade. A small group of men in army uniforms jumped from one of the parade vehicles and began firing submachine guns at Sadat's reviewing stand. Several other spectators were killed and more than 20 were wounded in the attack. Four men were captured at the scene and indicted, along with 20 others accused of aiding in the plot.

DON WRIGHT
Courtesy Miami News

JIM BORGMAN
Courtesy Cincinnati Enquirer

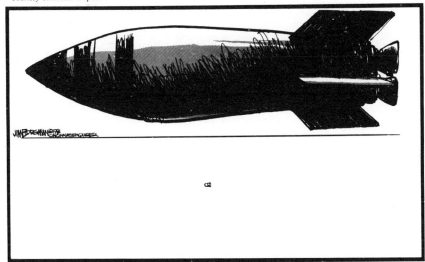

WHICH OF THESE POSES THE GREATER THREAT TO YOUR WORLD?

PAUL FELL
Courtesy Maverick Media

LARRY WRIGHT
Courtesy Detroit News

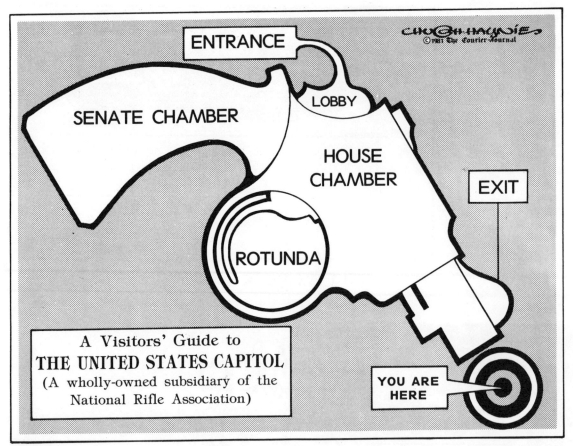

HUGH HAYNIE
Courtesy Louisville Courier–Journal

JIM MAZZOTTA
Ft. Myers News–Press

BILL DE ORE
Courtesy Dallas Morning News

JOSH BEUTEL
Courtesy St. John Telegraph-Journal

JON KENNEDY
Courtesy Arkansas Democrat

To attract a starlet

TOM ENGELHARDT
Courtesy St. Louis Post–Dispatch

ENGELHARDT
ST. LOUIS POST-DISPATCH

FRANK INTERLANDI
Courtesy Los Angeles Times

The American Way

CLIFF BALDOWSKI
Courtesy Atlanta Constitution

72

The Mideast

Just one hour after his inauguration as president, Ronald Reagan received word that the American hostages who had been held 444 days in Iran had been released. On January 25 the former hostages returned to the U.S. to a massive public welcome, including a parade up Pennsylvania Avenue and a White House reception.

Iran's war with Iraq remained stalemated, but Iran had major troubles at home. Its president, who had been in office only five weeks, and its prime minister were killed when a bomb exploded in a government building. Thousands of Iranians were killed by Khomeini's firing squads as political factions warred openly with each other.

OPEC oil prices remained depressed and Saudi Arabia successfully pushed for a two-dollar-per-barrel reduction.

On August 19 two U.S. Navy F-14 jets shot down two Soviet-built Libyan fighters about 60 miles off the Libyan coast after the American aircraft were attacked.

In Israel, Prime Minister Menachem Begin survived a close election to remain in office, but he was under frequent attack from those who opposed his policies.

MIKE PETERS
Courtesy Dayton Daily News

...THE HOSTAGES WERE FORCED TO SIT, DAY AFTER DAY, HUDDLED IN A SMALL ROOM.....SLEEPING ON BARE FLOORS...HUNGRY...WITH LITTLE OR NO FOOD...

TOM CURTIS
Courtesy Milwaukee Sentinel

"Repeat after me: Never again!"

ELDON PLETCHER
Courtesy New Orleans Times–Picayune

LAZARO FRESQUET
Courtesy El Miami Herald

"THE RETURN OF THE HOSTAGES"

CHUCK ASAY
Courtesy Colorado Springs Sun

RAY OSRIN
Courtesy Cleveland Plain Dealer

"...CAME THOSE RIBBONS, YELLOW RIBBONS, LOVELY RIBBONS FOR HER HAIR.."

VIC CANTONE
Courtesy New York Daily News

A FACE IN THE CROWD

EDD ULUSCHAK
Courtesy Edmonton Journal

CLIFF LEVERETTE
Courtesy Capitol Reporter (Miss.)

BILL GARNER
Courtesy Commercial Appeal (Memphis)

76

THE LAST IRANIAN

READY...AIM.....

CHARLES DANIEL
Courtesy Knoxville Journal

STEVE SACK
Courtesy Minneapolis Tribune

MIKE GRASTON
Courtesy Windsor Star (Ont.)

EYE OF THE BEHOLDER

SANDY CAMPBELL
Courtesy The Tennessean

ED FISCHER
Courtesy Rochester Post–Bulletin

LEW HARSH
Courtesy Scranton Times

ANDY DONATO
Courtesy Toronto Sun

CHUCK BROOKS
Courtesy Birmingham News

78

Linkage

DENNIS RENAULT
Courtesy Sacramento Bee

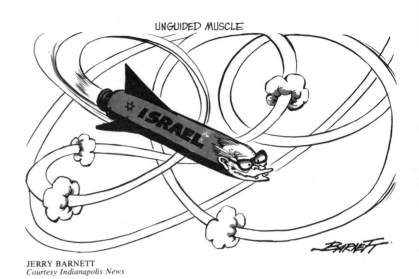

JERRY BARNETT
Courtesy Indianapolis News

JERRY FEARING
Courtesy St. Paul Dispatch–
Pioneer Press

79

DICK LOCHER
Courtesy Chicago Tribune

JERRY BARNETT
Courtesy Indianapolis News

Poland

The year 1981 brought extreme unrest and bitter economic hardship to beleaguered Poland. In early February, because he seemed unable to cope with workers' strikes, Jozef Pinkowski was dumped as premier and replaced by Gen. Wojciech Jaruzelski, Poland's fourth premier in less than a year. He appealed for a 90-day moratorium on strikes to give him time to work out differences with the Solidarity trade union.

There followed a brief period of calm, but in March four Solidarity supporters were beaten by police and further strikes were threatened. As unrest escalated, the economy continued to slide, and coal production fell more than 60 percent. Continuing shortages led to rationing of gasoline and tobacco, as well as meat and other basic foods.

In December labor militants proposed a referendum on the establishment of a noncommunist government and holding free elections. At that point the Soviet-controlled government drew the line. On December 13 martial law was imposed throughout Poland and thousands of activists were arrested, including Solidarity leader Lech Walesa. Poland's puppet government seemed to be doing all it could to deal with the problem so Soviet tanks would not come rumbling across the border.

JIM MAZZOTTA
Ft. Myers News–Press

ART HENRIKSON
© Paddock Publications

MICHAEL KONOPACKI
© Rothco and IUE News

TOM DARCY
Courtesy Newsday

FRANK EVERS
Courtesy New York Daily News

HOW FAR WILL IT STRETCH?

CLYDE PETERSON
Courtesy Houston Chronicle

DRAPER HILL
Courtesy Detroit News

Inflation

Interest rates were the big story in economic matters during 1981. The prime rate began the year at 21.5 percent, slipped slightly to around 17 percent for a time, but remained high throughout the twelve months. High interest was pinpointed as the chief culprit behind the stagnant economy. The construction industry suffered one of its worst years ever, as did the automobile industry, because of the high cost of borrowing money.

Inflation seemed to cool somewhat, however, as the Consumer Price Index held at around 8 to 9 percent much of the year. The restraint on money was cited as the primary reason. A large oil surplus also helped keep inflation from soaring as it had the previous year, and crude oil prices remained depressed.

JOHN TREVER
Courtesy Albuquerque Journal

"THE DRAPES STAY WITH THE HOUSE...."

Bank robbers

ERIC SMITH
Courtesy Capital–Gazette (Md.)

LOU GRANT
Courtesy Oakland Tribune

BRIAN BASSET
Courtesy Seattle Times

DANA SUMMERS
Courtesy Journal Herald (Ohio)

ETTA HULME
Courtesy Ft. Worth Star-Telegram

"I CAN WHIP ANY TAX CUT PLAN IN THE HOUSE"

EUGENE PAYNE
Courtesy Charlotte Observer

EDDIE GERMANO
Courtesy Brockton Daily Enterprise

TERRY MOSHER (AISLIN)
Courtesy Montreal Gazette

Access By Helicopter

JOSEPH HELLER
Courtesy West Bend News (Wisc.)

LATEST PICTURE

JIM DOBBINS
Courtesy Union-Leader

87

WALTER HANDELSMAN
Courtesy The Star (Md.)

EDD ULUSCHAK
Courtesy Edmonton Journal

"It was recalled . . . by the mortgage company."

STEVE SACK
Courtesy Minneapolis Tribune

WAYNE STAYSKAL
Courtesy Chicago Tribune

"GOOD NEWS... SOMEBODY STOLE OUR CAR!"

The Budget

Capitol Hill observers gave President Reagan's economic program little chances of passage when it first was presented to Congress, but the lawmakers ended up giving him exactly what he asked. Reagan had run on a pledge to cut taxes as well as federal spending. The final tax bill presented the American people with the largest tax cut in U.S. history—almost $750 billion spread over five years.

Immediately upon assuming office Reagan set out to remake the budget that had been proposed by outgoing president Jimmy Carter. Reagan called for higher defense outlays coupled with nondefense spending reductions, with the bulk of the savings to come from social welfare programs, public service jobs, and the food stamp program. School subsidies for meals for middle-class students were substantially reduced, although free lunches for the poor were continued. Loans for college and trade school students also were cut back.

As 1981 ended, Reagan had all but given up hope that he would be able to offer a balanced budget for 1984 as he had promised during the presidential campaign. The budget deficit for 1981 climbed to $55.2 billion.

BOB TAYLOR
Courtesy Dallas Times–Herald

JOHN COLLINS
Courtesy Montreal Gazette

ETTA HULME
Courtesy Ft. Worth Star–Telegram

KEN ALEXANDER
Courtesy San Francisco Examiner

"Sir Ronald, many a fair knight has sought yon Holy Grail . . . don't hold thy breath"

BOB ZSCHIESCHE
Courtesy Our Folks

BRIAN BASSET
Courtesy Seattle Times

BEN SARGENT
Courtesy Austin American–Statesman

JOHN MILT MORRIS
©The Associated Press

BOB ARTLEY
*Courtesy Worthington (Minn.)
Daily Globe*

How much pruning can we do and still get apples?

DENNIS RENAULT
Courtesy Sacramento Bee

'Put him back on the block; I'm not through yet!'

JIMMY MARGULIES
©Rothco

"IF YOU HAVE A VALET TO PARK HIS SLED, A FEW ACRES TO GRAZE THE REINDEER, AND A JACUZZI TO HELP HIM UNWIND, MAYBE SANTA WILL VISIT YOU THIS YEAR."

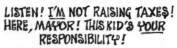

BILL SANDERS
Courtesy Milwaukee Journal

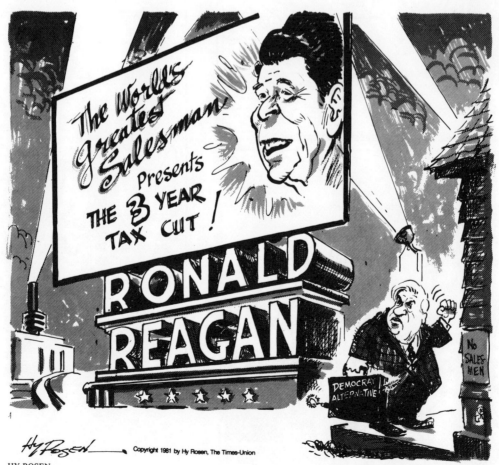

HY ROSEN
Courtesy Albany Times–Union

'Jelly Beans?'

SANDY CAMPBELL
Courtesy The Tennessean

VIC CANTONE
Courtesy New York Daily News

REAGANOMICS

ED STEIN
Courtesy Rocky Mountain News

JERRY DOYLE
Courtesy Philadelphia Daily News

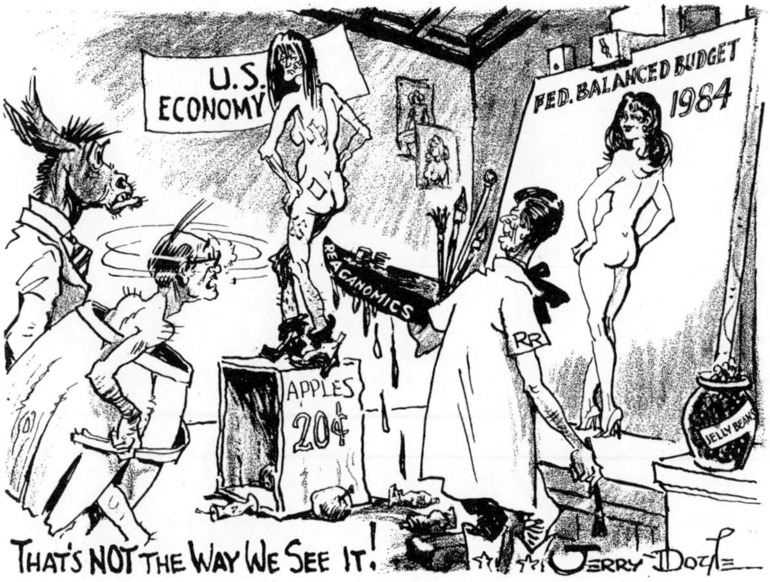
U.S. ECONOMY
FED. BALANCED BUDGET 1984
REAGANOMICS
APPLES 20¢
JELLY BEANS
RR
THAT'S NOT THE WAY WE SEE IT!
JERRY DOYLE

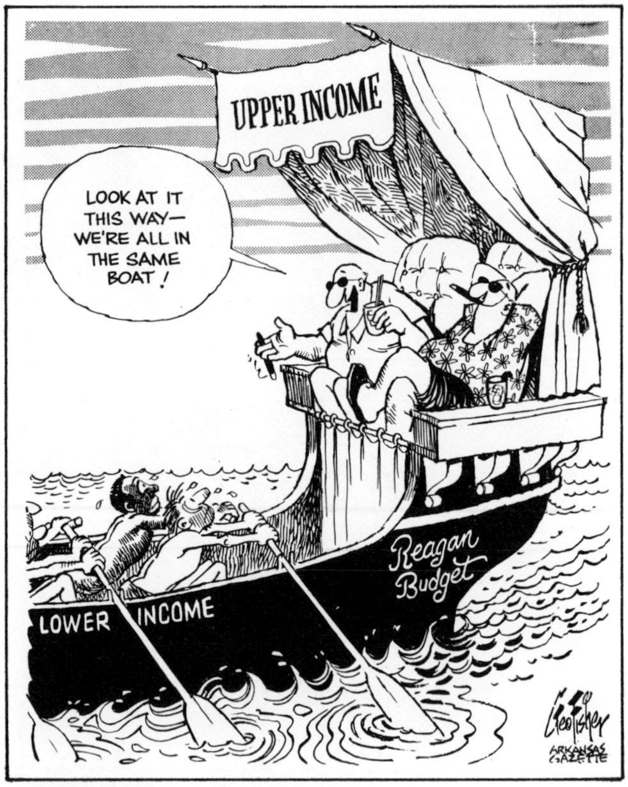
UPPER INCOME
LOOK AT IT THIS WAY— WE'RE ALL IN THE SAME BOAT!
Reagan Budget
LOWER INCOME
ARKANSAS GAZETTE

GEORGE FISHER
Courtesy Arkansas Gazette

TIM MENEES
Courtesy Pittsburgh Post-Gazette

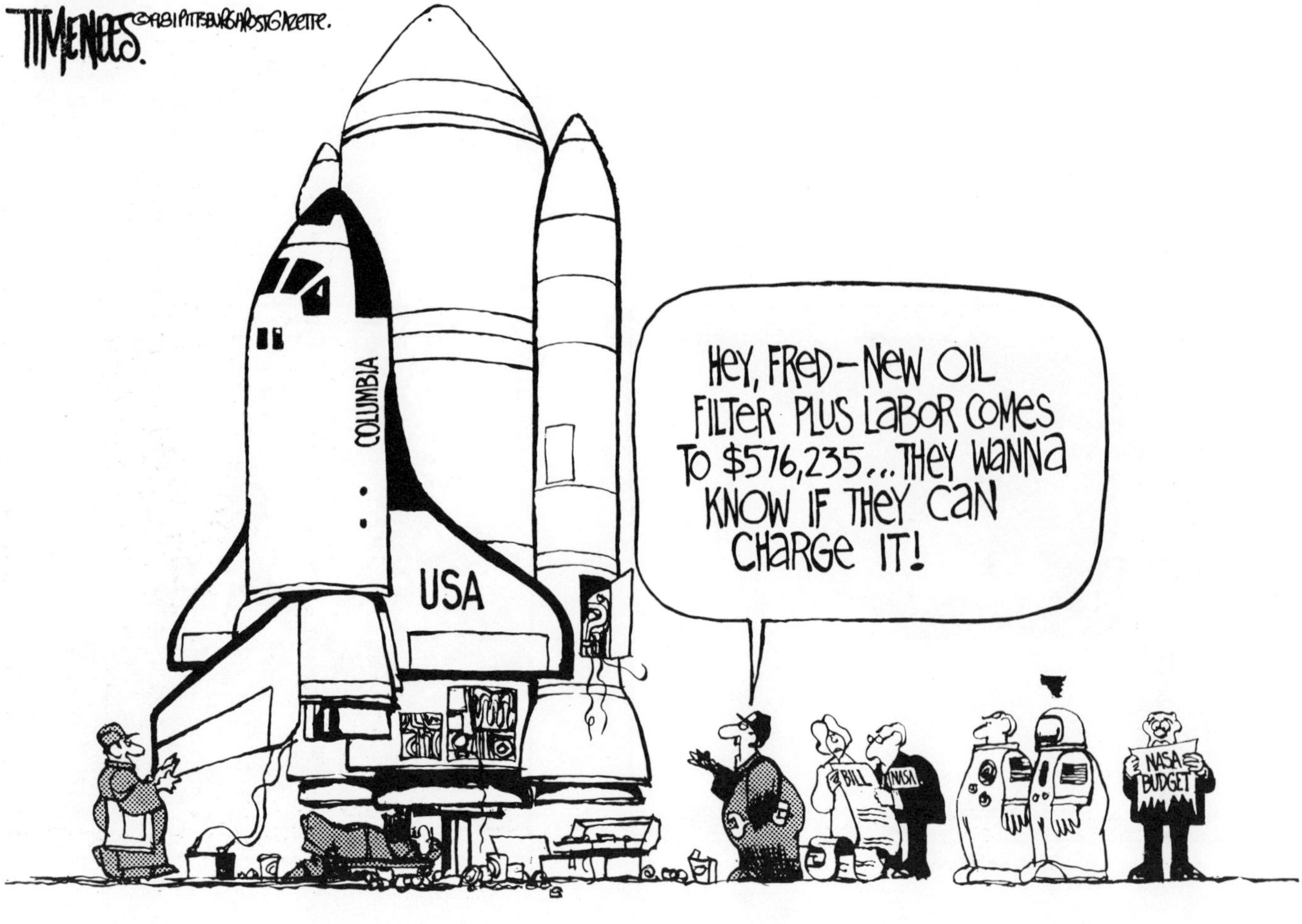
TIM MENEES ©1981 PITTSBURGH POST-GAZETTE.
COLUMBIA
USA
HEY, FRED—NEW OIL FILTER PLUS LABOR COMES TO $576,235... THEY WANNA KNOW IF THEY CAN CHARGE IT!
BILL
NASA
NASA BUDGET

David Stockman

David Stockman, appointed director of the Office of Management and Budget by President Reagan, was the youngest person to hold cabinet rank in more than 150 years. He had been Reagan's main spokesman on budget matters and was looked upon by liberals as a hard-hearted hatchet man because of his numerous cuts in social programs.

Toward the end of the year, an article in *The Atlantic Monthly* based on a series of interviews with Stockman caused a mighty furor. Stockman admitted in the article that he had never really believed the administration's supply-side economic policies could work without huge budget deficits. He declared that the large tax cuts that had been pushed through Congress had been a "Trojan horse" which gave tax breaks primarily to the rich.

His credibility, of course, was damaged, and even staunch Reagan supporters demanded that he be fired. Stockman apologized to the President and offered to resign, but Reagan kept him on the job.

FRANK EVERS
Courtesy New York Daily News

DAVEY STOCKMAN TOOK AN AX
AND GAVE THE BUDGET 40 WHACKS.
WHEN HE SAW WHAT HE HAD DONE,
HE GAVE THE WHITE HOUSE 41.

MIKE JENKINS
Courtesy Beaumont Enterprise

JACK MCLEOD
Courtesy Buffalo Evening News

BOB ARTLEY
Courtesy Worthington (Minn.)
Daily Globe

The emperor's new clothes — (or, The truth will ouch)

KARL HUBENTHAL
Courtesy Los Angeles Herald–Examiner

CHARLES DANIEL
Courtesy Knoxville Journal

TIM MENEES
Courtesy Pittsburgh Post–Gazette

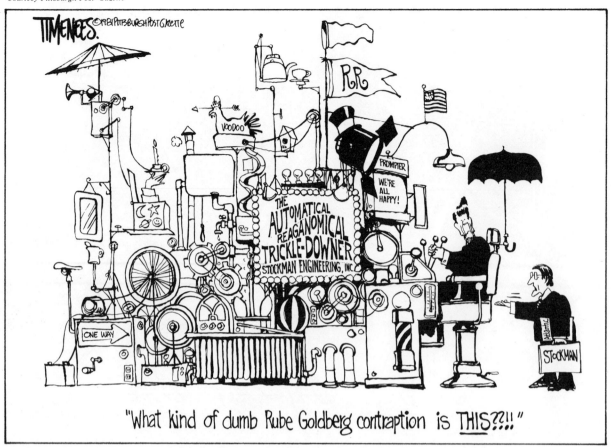

"What kind of dumb Rube Goldberg contraption is THIS??!!"

JIMMY JOHNSON
Courtesy Jackson (Miss.) Daily News

"DON'T LOOK NOW, BUT YOUR DOCTOR JUST SCREWED UP BAD."

DWANE POWELL
Courtesy News & Observer (N.C.)

JIM BERRY
©NEA

"That little giggle of yours is a dead giveaway that you've found MORE cuts to be made in social programs."

BRUCE PLANTE
Courtesy Fayetteville Times (N.C.)

101

The Supreme Court

President Reagan delivered on one of his major campaign promises on July 7 when he named Sandra Day O'Connor to a seat on the U. S. Supreme Court. The first woman ever to be appointed to that panel, O'Connor received a 99 to 0 confirmation from the Senate and took her place on the Court on September 25. Her only opposition had come from conservatives who were dissatisfied with her record on abortion and the Equal Rights Amendment.

At the time of her appointment, O'Connor was a judge on the Arizona Court of Appeals. She had earned a law degree at Stanford University and finished in the top 10 percent of her class.

In a speech to young lawyers near the end of 1981 Chief Justice Warren Burger came down hard on the need for swift justice for criminals. He contended that too many judges were soft on lawbreakers and that the trial process should be speeded up.

JIM BORGMAN
Courtesy Cincinnati Enquirer

"WELL, AT LEAST IT'LL BE CHEAPER THAN IF HE'D HIRED A MAN..."

KARL HUBENTHAL
Courtesy Los Angeles Herald–Examiner

JON KENNEDY
Courtesy Arkansas Democrat

' —Just a minute! I've changed my mind'

BERT WHITMAN
Courtesy Phoenix Gazette

LEW HARSH
Courtesy Scranton Times

EUGENE CRAIG
Courtesy Columbus Dispatch

CHUCK ASAY
Courtesy Colorado Springs Sun

DON WRIGHT
Courtesy Miami News

Women's Rights

The proposed Equal Rights Amendment must receive ratification by 38 states by June 30, 1982, or it will die aborning. For the past four years, the number of ratifying states has stood at 35.

Some of the earlier ratifications are now in doubt because in several cases state legislatures have voted to repeal their earlier approval. As the year ended, proponents of the bill were readying an all-out effort to save the ERA.

Controversy continued during the year over the issue of abortion. Congress came under increased pressure to overturn a 1973 Supreme Court decision that recognized abortion as an individual right.

ETTA HULME
Courtesy Ft. Worth Star-Telegram

THE MILWAUKEE JOURNAL

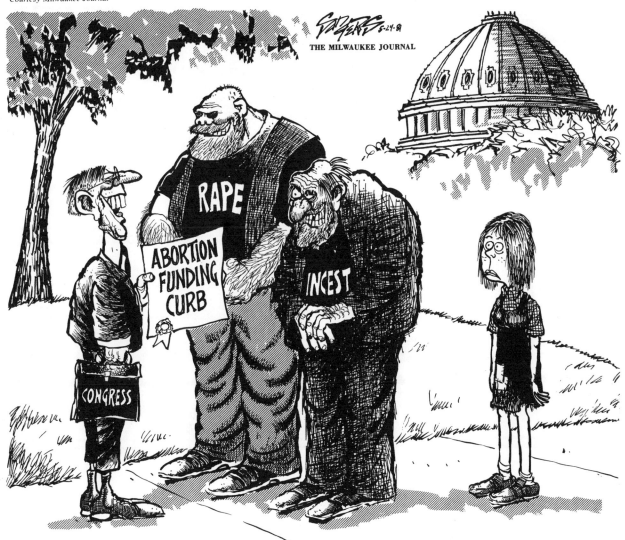

'Here's your license to produce babies!'

"Paradoxically, I'm also pro handgun, pro cigarette smoking, pro arms race, and pro wipeout social programs."

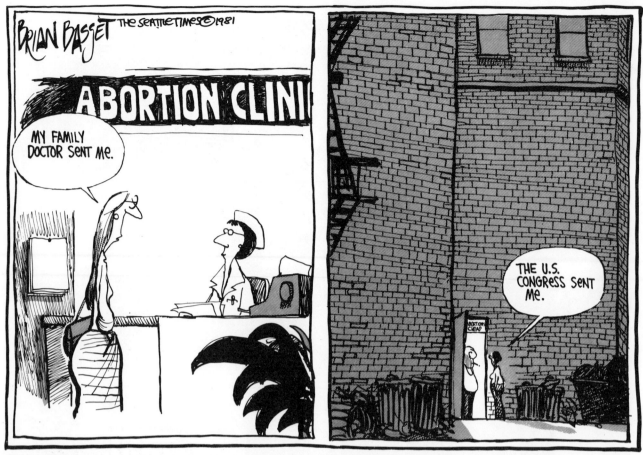

BRIAN BASSET
Courtesy Seattle Times

RAY OSRIN
Courtesy Cleveland Plain Dealer

"WHEN DOES LIFE BEGIN? I'LL TELL YOU WHEN LIFE BEGINS. MY FELLOW DOCTORS, LIFE BEGINS WHEN THE CHILDREN MOVE OUT!"

Anwar Sadat

Egyptian President Anwar Sadat was assassinated in Cairo on October 6 while viewing a military parade. As Sadat and other dignitaries watched a display of Mirage jet fighters in the sky, a small band of men wearing military uniforms leaped from one of the parade vehicles and began firing with submachine guns at point-blank range.

Sadat was rushed by helicopter to a military hospital where he died two hours later from multiple bullet wounds. Several spectators in the reviewing stand were killed and more than 20 others were wounded. The four assassins were captured at the scene and were later tried and convicted.

Sadat had won the 1978 Nobel Peace Prize, sharing it with Israel's prime minister, Menachem Begin. Sadat was widely regarded, both in the United States and around the world, as a great statesman in quest of peace. In the eyes of many Arabs, however, he was considered a traitor because of concessions he had made in search of peace in the Mideast.

Giant Footprints In The Sands of Time

CHARLES BISSELL
Courtesy The Tennessean

PAUL CONRAD
Courtesy Los Angeles Times

JIM MORGAN
Courtesy Spartanburg Herald–Journal

THE FOURTH WISEMAN

HY ROSEN
Courtesy Albany Times–Union

LADY IN THE DARK

EGYPT WITHOUT ANWAR SADAT

MIDEAST PEACE HOPES

BERT WHITMAN
Courtesy Phoenix Gazette

DAVID WILEY MILLER
©Copley News Service

And I had done an hellish thing
  And it would work 'em woe:
For all averr'd, I had killed the Bird
  That made the Breeze to blow.
The Ancient Mariner

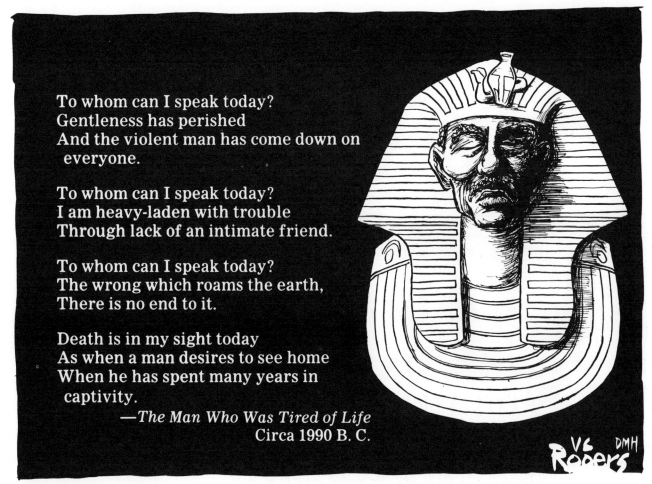

To whom can I speak today?
Gentleness has perished
And the violent man has come down on
  everyone.

To whom can I speak today?
I am heavy-laden with trouble
Through lack of an intimate friend.

To whom can I speak today?
The wrong which roams the earth,
There is no end to it.

Death is in my sight today
As when a man desires to see home
When he has spent many years in
  captivity.
          —*The Man Who Was Tired of Life*
                    Circa 1990 B. C.

V. CULLUM ROGERS
Courtesy Durham Morning Herald

BLAINE
Courtesy The Spectator (Ont.)

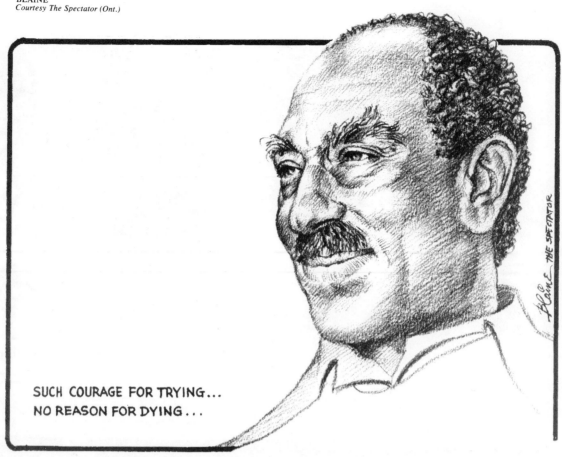

SUCH COURAGE FOR TRYING...
NO REASON FOR DYING...

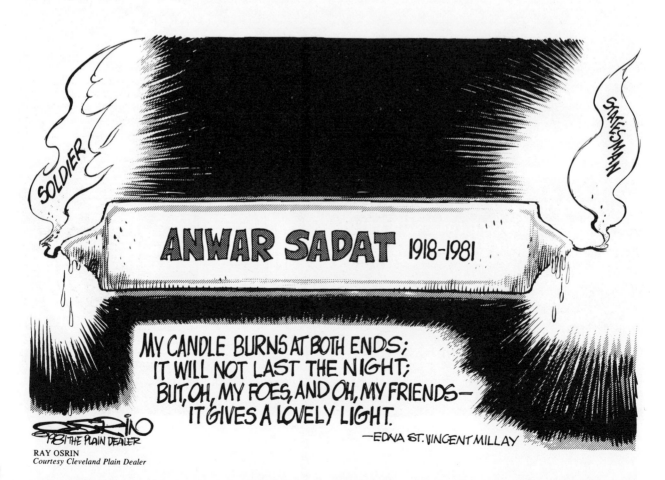

SOLDIER

STATESMAN

ANWAR SADAT 1918-1981

MY CANDLE BURNS AT BOTH ENDS;
IT WILL NOT LAST THE NIGHT;
BUT, OH, MY FOES, AND OH, MY FRIENDS—
IT GIVES A LOVELY LIGHT.
—EDNA ST. VINCENT MILLAY

RAY OSRIN
Courtesy Cleveland Plain Dealer

Controllers' Strike

One of the most pivotal labor strikes in history occurred on August 3 when members of the Professional Air Traffic Controllers Organization (PATCO) walked off their jobs. In spite of the fact that their salaries ranged from $20,500 to $50,000 per year, the union demanded some $700 million in improved benefits. A package had been worked out earlier by PATCO head Robert E. Poli and U. S. Secretary of Transportation Drew Lewis which would have given an average raise of $4,000 per controller. The agreement was rejected by rank and file members.

When PATCO went out on strike, President Reagan urged them to return to work, emphasizing that it is illegal for government workers to strike. He then issued the controllers an ultimatum to return to work within 48 hours or be fired. Some 12,000 of the 16,000 working controllers refused to work and Reagan fired them.

Late in the year PATCO was decertified as a union, and shortly thereafter Poli resigned his position.

DICK WALLMEYER
Courtesy Independent Press–Telegram
    (Calif.)

ED FISCHER
Courtesy Rochester Post–Bulletin

OF COURSE WE'LL BRING YOU IN SAFELY, FLIGHT 507...... FOR TEN GRAND...

MIKE MORGAN
Courtesy Macon Telegraph & News

COLLISION COURSE

JIM LANGE
Courtesy Daily Oklahoman

"PATCO TO PASSENGERS, 'GO TO H___'"

JIM DOBBINS
Courtesy Union–Leader

ROY CARLESS
Courtesy Steel Labor, VE News

OVERKILL

JON KENNEDY
Courtesy Arkansas Democrat

'Can't we sit down and talk this over!'

VERN THOMPSON
Courtesy Lawton (Okla.) Constitution

115

LEMMINGS

CHUCK BROOKS
Courtesy Birmingham News

MICHAEL KONOPACKI
©Rothco and IUE News

FOR THE IUE NEWS
KONOPACKI

pateo ON STRIKE

SOLIDARNOSĆ STRAJK

"MY GOVERNMENT'S A DEMOCRACY. WHAT'S YOURS?"

1981 © THE SEATTLE TIMES   BRIAN BASSET

ROBERT POLI

AIR TRAFFIC CONTROL

THE AYAPOLI

BRIAN BASSET
Courtesy Seattle Times

116

DRAPER HILL
Courtesy Detroit News

VIC RUNTZ
Courtesy Bangor Daily News

The new controller

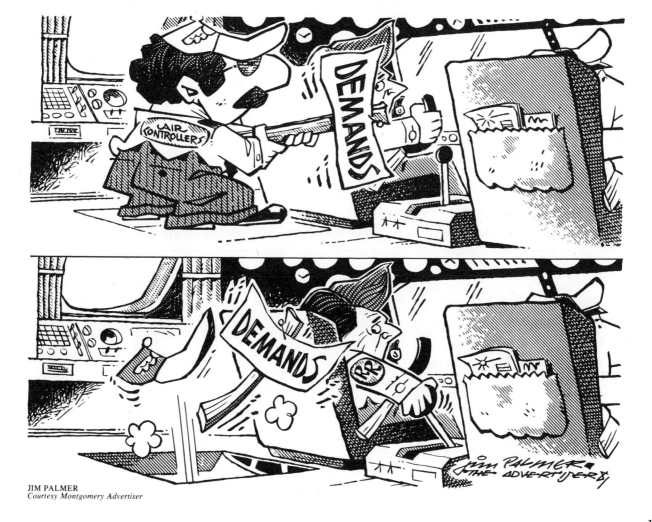

JIM PALMER
Courtesy Montgomery Advertiser

DANA SUMMERS
Courtesy Journal Herald (Ohio)

JIM LARRICK
Courtesy Clarion–Ledger (Miss.)

SAM RAWLS
Courtesy Atlanta Journal

The Press

The credibility of the press, and of certain newspapers, was dealt a severe blow in 1981. In April the 17-member Pulitzer Prize Advisory Board overruled the recommendations of one of its panel of judges and awarded the feature reporting prize to Janet Cooke, a 26-year-old reporter for *The Washington Post*. Her winning story was about an eight-year-old heroin addict in Washington's black ghetto.

Shortly after the announcement of the award, however, the colleges from which Cooke said she had earned degrees stated she had not done so. At first, Cooke stood by her story, but later admitted she had concocted most of it. The *Post* accepted her resignation and the prize was withdrawn. In a journalistic *mea culpa,* the *Post* published a column criticizing its own editors for not checking the facts of the story before publication.

On March 26 a jury in Los Angeles County Superior Court ruled that the *National Enquirer* must pay actress Carol Burnett $1.6 million because she had been libeled by the publication. The article in question implied that Miss Burnett had been intoxicated in public, an allegation she denied. The trial was watched closely by other celebrities, who may also bring suits against tabloids that lean toward journalistic sensationalism.

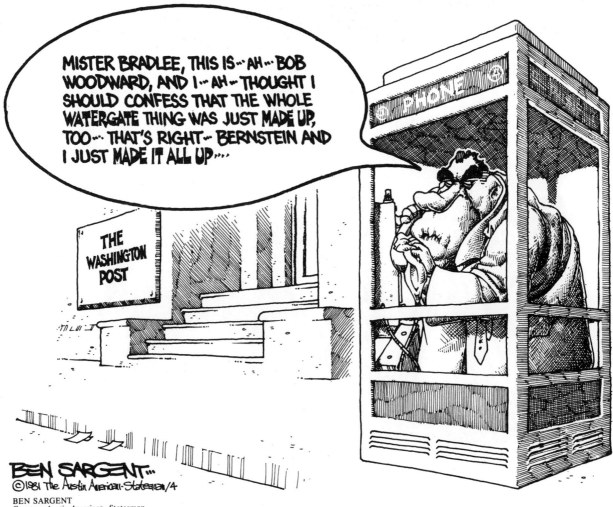

BEN SARGENT
Courtesy Austin American–Statesman

DAVID SATTLER
Courtesy Lafayette (Ind.) Journal and Courier

CHAN LOWE
Courtesy Oklahoma City Times

DOUGLAS BORGSTEDT
©Editor and Publisher

The 4th Estate

NEWS HOLE

"MR. BRADLEE, I GOT THREE SOURCES FOR THAT OBITUARY... HERE'S THE GUY WHO BURIED HIM, THE MINISTER AT THE FUNERAL AND THE DEAD MAN'S BROTHER.!!!"

CHAN LOWE
Courtesy Oklahoma City Times

CLIFF BALDOWSKI
Courtesy Atlanta Constitution

DOUGLAS BORGSTEDT
©Editor and Publisher

Canadian Politics

One of Canada's hottest political issues during the year revolved around the nation's constitution and how to amend it without help from Great Britain. Prime Minister Pierre Trudeau faced other problems as well, such as reactions to his energy policies and a stagnant economy.

Trudeau assigned great importance to the idea of "patriation" of the Canadian constitution. The document itself is actually kept in the House of Lords in London, where it is referred to as the British North American Act of 1867. More than four years ago the British offered to relinquish authority over Canadian constitutional law, but the Canadians have been unable to agree on how they would go about making constitutional amendments.

Trudeau and the provinces' premiers did not see eye to eye on how best to accomplish this objective, but they finally reached a compromise that included an amendment formula favored by the premiers and a national bill of rights Trudeau had endorsed. Quebec premier Rene Levesque, however, refused to sign the agreement.

Inflation remained a troublesome problem, closing the year at about 13 percent, while the unemployment rate hovered around 7 percent.

Acid rain made up of gases emitted from American industrial plants and automobiles was believed responsible for killing wildlife in Canada's high-altitude lake areas. Proposals were advanced to force plants in the east and midwest to reduce emissions of sulfur oxide.

RAOUL HUNTER
Courtesy Le Soleil (Que.)

RAOUL HUNTER
Courtesy Le Soleil (Que.)

ANDY DONATO
Courtesy Toronto Sun

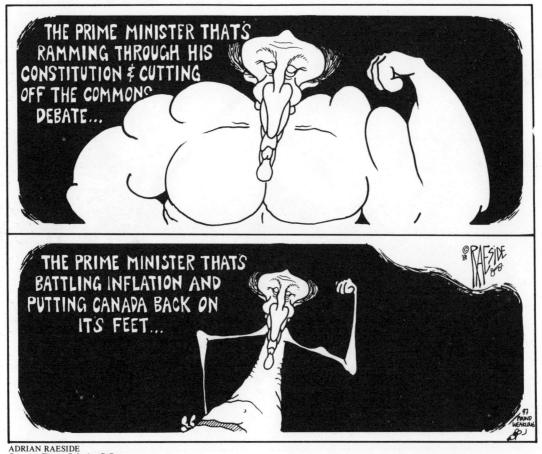

ADRIAN RAESIDE
Courtesy Times–Colonist (B.C.)

MERLE TINGLEY
Courtesy London Free Press (Can.)

JOHN COLLINS
Courtesy Montreal Gazette

IF AT FIRST YOU DON'T SECEDE...

ROY CARLESS
Courtesy Steel Labor, VE News

'IF YOU THINK YOU'RE IN HOT WATER NOW, WAIT 'TIL YOU GET HOME!'

The Royal Wedding

A ceremony reflecting the pomp and spectacle of a storybook fantasy took place in St. Paul's Cathedral in London on July 29 when Prince Charles married Lady Diana Spencer. Nearly 2,500 guests witnessed the wedding inside the church while another one million gathered along the processional route. Still another estimated 750 million television viewers around the world watched the event.

Charles, heir to the British throne, was married in full military uniform and Diana wore a striking ivory silk taffeta gown, the design of which had been a closely guarded secret prior to the actual ceremony.

The couple had announced their engagement in late February.

WAYNE STAYSKAL
Courtesy Chicago Tribune

MIKE GRASTON
Courtesy Windsor Star (Ont.)

JIM LANGE
Courtesy Daily Oklahoman

HY ROSEN
Courtesy Albany Times-Union

JERRY BARNETT
Courtesy Indianapolis News

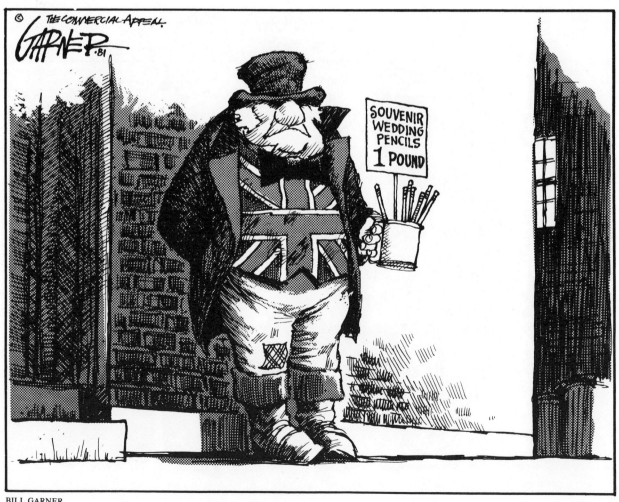

BILL GARNER
Courtesy Commercial Appeal (Memphis)

Baseball Strike

Major league baseball players staged a strike on June 12—despite the fact that their salaries averaged $173,000 annually—and they stayed out for 50 days. More than 700 games were canceled and the players lost some $28 million in salaries. Losses of the team owners were minimized by a $50 million strike insurance policy underwritten by Lloyd's of London and by a $15 million strike fund.

The dispute centered on free-agent compensation, and the eventual settlement increased the obligations of teams that signed free agents.

RICHARD CROWSON
Courtesy Jackson (Tenn.) Sun

JOHN TREVER
Courtesy Albuquerque Journal

BOB ZSCHIESCHE
Courtesy Our Folks

DICK WALLMEYER
Courtesy Independent Press–Telegram
   (Calif.)

ROB LAWLOR
Courtesy Philadelphia Daily News

SCOTT WILLIS
Courtesy Cleveland Press

"...THERE'LL BE A SLIGHT DELAY, SPORTSFANS, APPARENTLY ONE OF THE
VENDORS DROPPED A QUARTER AND IT ROLLED ONTO THE FIELD.."

DWANE POWELL
Courtesy News & Observer (N.C.)

ELDON PLETCHER
Courtesy New Orleans Times–Picayune

JIMMY MARGULIES
©Rothco

The Environment

The year brought a dramatic change in federal management of the nation's resources. Environmental regulations were sharply reduced, and the extraction of oil and coal was actively encouraged by the Reagan Administration. Secretary of the Interior James Watt caught most of the criticism for these moves, particularly when he opened up wilderness areas and a billion acres of offshore tracts for oil and gas leasing.

Acid rain apparently killed large numbers of wildlife in about half of the high-altitude lakes in the mountains of northeastern New York State. Many other lakes in the northeastern U. S. and eastern Canada may also have been harmed by this polluted rain.

The Reagan Administration held firm to a general policy of rolling back environmental regulations for industry. Industry was allowed more time to clean up waste because of the immense cost involved. In addition, requirements for cleaning the water and air were not as stringently enforced as environmentalists had demanded.

PAUL DUGINSKI
Courtesy Sacramento Union

The Administration's Pollution Solution:

1 Air Pollution Controls are relaxed so that cars produce more pollutants

2 Acid Rain clouds are formed

3 Polluting automobiles are slowly dissolved

SIZZLE SIZZLE

KEEFE THE DENVER POST '81

MIKE KEEFE
Courtesy Denver Post

PAUL CONRAD
Courtesy Los Angeles Times

DIABLO CANYON LIGHTHOUSE

MIKE PETERS
Courtesy Dayton Daily News

Really Grim fairy tales by JAMES WATT

©1981 DAYTON DAILY NEWS

...THEN ONE DAY THE BRAVE AND HANDSOME HUNTER CAME UPON A CLEARING IN A WOODED GLADE...SUDDENLY HE RAISED HIS TRUSTY RIFLE AND TOOK CAREFUL AIM... BLAM, BLAM... HE DROPPED BAMBI AND BAMBI'S MOTHER... BLAM, BLAM... HE GOT THUMPER AND FLOWER... BLAM, BLAM, BLAM...

JERRY FEARING
*Courtesy St. Paul Dispatch–
Pioneer Press*

ROGER HARVELL
Courtesy Pine Bluff Commercial

TOM ENGELHARDT
Courtesy St. Louis Post–Dispatch

'Your Wish Is My Command'

JOHN COLLINS
Courtesy Montreal Gazette

STEVE GREENBERG
Courtesy Los Angeles Daily News

DOUBLE, DOUBLE TOIL AND TROUBLE;
FIRE BURN AND CAULDRON BUBBLE.

TOXIC WASTE AND PCBs
BRING ON SUFFERING AND DISEASE;
ACID RAIN AND NUCLEAR SPILLS
INFECT ALL WITH ASSORTED ILLS.
LEACH INTO THE LAKE AND RIVER,
POISON BOTH THE LUNG AND LIVER.
SPREAD THIS WASTE
  UPON THE LAND,
INTO THE FLESH
  OF CHILD AND MAN.

BY THE DAMAGE
  MAN HAS DONE,
SOMETHING WICKED
  THIS WAY COMES.

STEIN '81
ROCKY MTN.
NEWS ·NEA

ED STEIN
Courtesy Rocky Mountain News

"IT'S THE STATE D.E.P. CHECKING AS TO WHETHER
WE'RE CONCERNED ABOUT THE POTENTIALLY DANGEROUS
WASTE DUMP NEARBY...WHAT SHOULD I TELL HIM?"

BOB BECKETT
Courtesy WCAU-TV (Phila.)

DAVID HORSEY
Courtesy Seattle Post–Intelligencer

136

The Med Fly

The Mediterranean fruit fly swarmed into California in the spring, threatening the state's huge vegetable and fruit crops. The state legislature pressed for the use of aerial spraying, but Governor Jerry Brown declined to act, insisting that such spraying might create a health hazard.

U. S. Secretary of Agriculture John R. Block got Brown's attention by threatening to quarantine Californian produce if the Med fly was not brought under control. Brown finally agreed to aerial spraying in three counties, but by mid-August the insect had reached the lush San Joaquin Valley, the heart of California's agricultural industry. By mid-September the quarantined area had been extended to include 4,000 square miles, and the state expected to spend $100 million on an eradication program that stretched into the fall.

Governor Brown's political future was not enhanced by the Med fly episode. Polls showed that 60 percent of his constituents were critical of his handling of the problem.

KEN ALEXANDER
Courtesy San Francisco Examiner

LOU GRANT
Courtesy Oakland Tribune

BILL GARNER
Courtesy Commercial Appeal (Memphis)

EDGAR SOLLER
Courtesy Bataan News/Filipino
  American

JIM DOBBINS
Courtesy Union–Leader

KARL HUBENTHAL
Courtesy Los Angeles Herald–Examiner

JIM BERRY
©NEA

ED ASHLEY
Courtesy Toledo Blade

PAUL DUGINSKI
Courtesy Sacramento Union

DAVID SATTLER
*Courtesy Lafayette (Ind.) Journal and
Courier*

"ISN'T IT AMAZING HOW QUICKLY A STATE CAN RESPOND TO A CRISIS"

CHARLES DANIEL
Courtesy Knoxville Journal

The Moral Majority

The Reverend Jerry Falwell of the Moral Majority and the Reverend Donald E. Wildman of the National Federation for Decency formed the Coalition for Better Television during 1981. They threatened to lead a massive boycott of products that supported television programs featuring sex and violence.

The chairman of the board of Proctor and Gamble, one of television's largest advertisers, indicated in June that his company also found some television programs objectionable. His statement created ripples throughout the industry, and the coalition called off the proposed boycott. Nevertheless, the leaders said they would maintain a monitoring program to keep the pressure on advertisers.

The Moral Majority continued to grow during the year, claiming a mailing list membership of more than 400,000 and chapters in all 50 states.

The Moral Majority received criticism, as well. The Reverend Billy Graham chided Falwell for not addressing such issues as social injustice and the arms race. Senator Barry Goldwater, once a leading conservative, accused Falwell's group of violating the principle of separation of church and state.

PAUL CONRAD
Courtesy Los Angeles Times

ETTA HULME
Courtesy Ft. Worth Star–Telegram

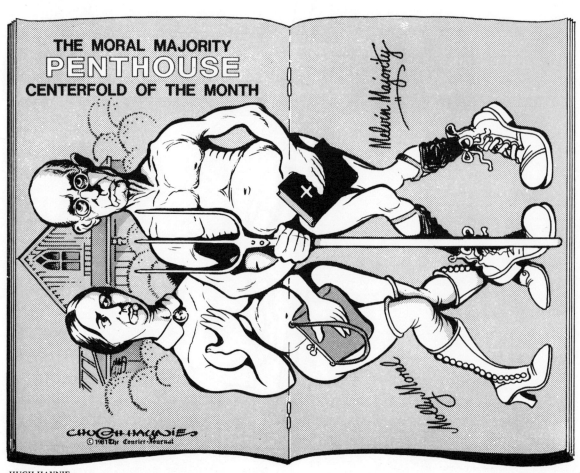

HUGH HAYNIE
Courtesy Louisville Courier–Journal

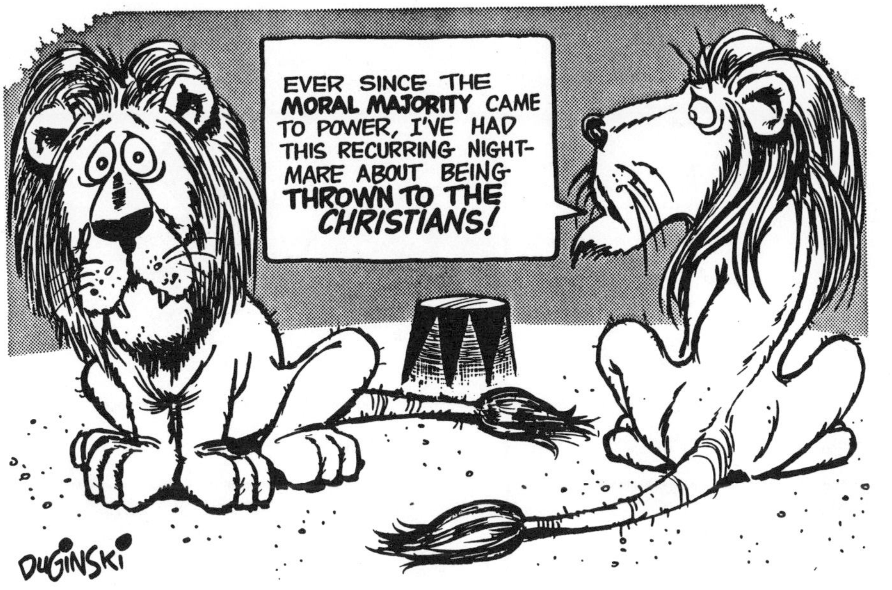
EVER SINCE THE MORAL MAJORITY CAME TO POWER, I'VE HAD THIS RECURRING NIGHT-MARE ABOUT BEING THROWN TO THE CHRISTIANS!
DUGINSKI

PAUL DUGINSKI
Courtesy Sacramento Union

SAM RAWLS
Courtesy Atlanta Journal

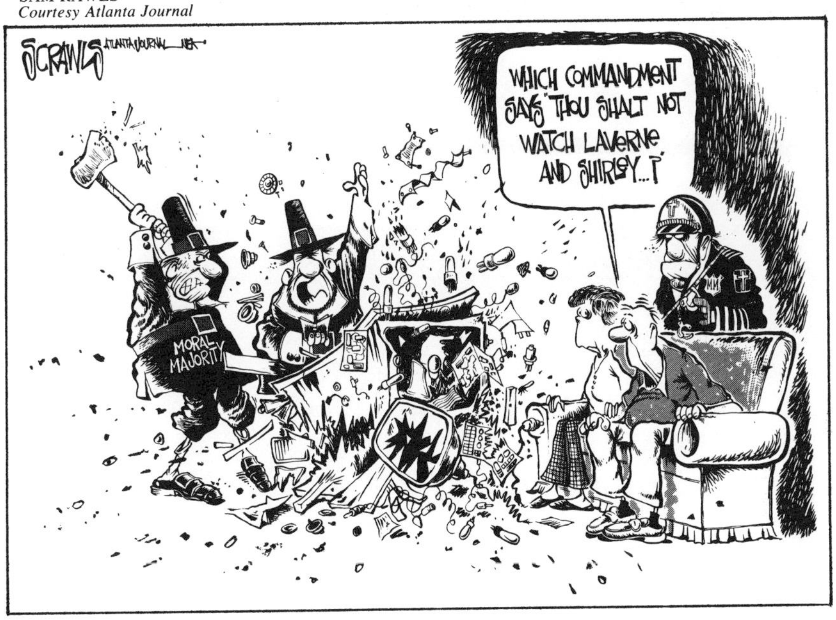
SCRAWLS
WHICH COMMANDMENT SAYS "THOU SHALT NOT WATCH LAVERNE AND SHIRLEY...?"
MORAL MAJORITY

JIM LARRICK
Courtesy Clarion–Ledger (Miss.)

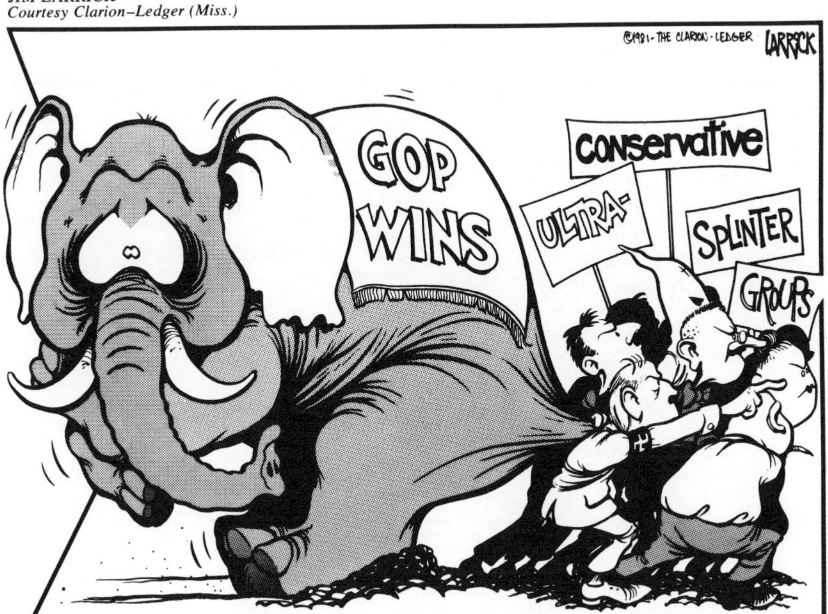
©1981 - THE CLARION - LEDGER
LARRICK
GOP WINS
conservative
ULTRA-
SPLINTER
GROUPS
"RIGHT! RIGHT! RIGHT-ON!"

BILL DE ORE
Courtesy Dallas Morning News

MIKE KEEFE
Courtesy Denver Post

HY ROSEN
Courtesy Albany Times–Union

Richard Nixon

At the request of President Reagan, former president Richard Nixon joined Gerald Ford and Jimmy Carter, the other two living ex-presidents, to represent the U. S. at Egyptian president Anwar Sadat's funeral in Cairo in early October.

Nixon was also in the news because of a squabble at Duke University in Durham, North Carolina. The university's president had proposed that the Richard M. Nixon Presidential Library be housed on the campus, drawing cries of outrage from some quarters. The facility would contain records from the Nixon Administration, including the famous Watergate tapes.

V. CULLUM ROGERS
Courtesy Durham Morning Herald

JACK JURDEN
Courtesy Wilmington Evening
Journal–News

RICHARD MILHOUS NINELIVES

LOU GRANT
Courtesy Oakland Tribune

© 1981 Los Angeles Times Syndicate

JACK MCLEOD
Courtesy Buffalo Evening News

ROB LAWLOR
Courtesy Philadelphia Daily News

VIC RUNTZ
Courtesy Bangor Daily News

The scary part

. . . and Other Issues

As the crime rate in the U. S. continued to rise, the problem of over-crowded prisons became more acute. In Alabama a federal court order released 222 inmates in an attempt to relieve overcrowded conditions. Georgia has been under a court order since 1978 to reduce its prison population. In spite of early releases, however, the number of prisoners reached an all-time high. In state after state similar problems confronted officials.

There was a series of deaths in Ireland from hunger strikes undertaken by supporters of the Irish Republican Army, an underground organization that seeks autonomy for the country.

Spectacular discoveries about the solar system were still being made from photographs and measurements taken by Voyager II, which rocketed within 63,000 miles of Saturn on August 25. The colorful, detailed photographs showed that Saturn's rings are more complex than had been believed.

On November 28 at Legion Field in Birmingham, Paul "Bear" Bryant became the "winningest" coach in college football when his University of Alabama team defeated Auburn. Bryant achieved the distinction in his 37th year of coaching.

In March the domestic first-class mail rate rose to 18 cents and in November was increased again to 20 cents. Further rate increases appeared to be on the way.

BEN SARGENT
Courtesy Austin American–Statesman

LARRY WRIGHT
Courtesy Detroit News

CHARLES BISSELL
Courtesy The Tennessean

Neither Snow, Nor Rain, Nor Heat, Nor Gloom of Night Stays
THESE Couriers From The Swift Completion of Their Appointed Rounds

JOHN BRANCH
Courtesy San Antonio Express–News

BILL DE ORE
Courtesy Dallas Morning News

"THREE HUNDRED YEARS TOO LATE!!"

JIM LANGE
Courtesy Daily Oklahoman

MIKE PETERS
Courtesy Dayton Daily News

JOHN CRAWFORD
Courtesy Alabama Journal

"IF YOU ARE RELEASED BECAUSE OF OVERCROWDING...YOU BETTER COME STRAIGHT HOME!"

JACK BENDER
Courtesy Waterloo Courier

WAYNE STAYSKAL
Courtesy Chicago Tribune

"HARRY 'MAD DOG' McDUMM, I SENTENCE YOU TO THE FIRST AVAILABLE VACANCY IN THE STATE PENITENTIARY!"

DOUG REGALIA
Courtesy Daily Californian

"THE PENDULUM OF JUSTICE"

BOB TAYLOR
Courtesy Dallas Times Herald

FRANK INTERLANDI
Courtesy Los Angeles Times

TOM DARCY
Courtesy Newsday

'Travelers come to surf, play, and forget their everyday problems.
—Florida Tourist Dept.

ED STEIN
Courtesy Rocky Mountain News

JIM MORGAN
Courtesy Spartanburg Herald–Journal

THE RINGS OF VOYAGER II

CLYDE PETERSON
Courtesy Houston Chronicle

One lands, one soars

THERE'VE BEEN SOME CHANGES MADE!

ART WOOD
Courtesy AFBF (Md.)

Born Again

REG MANNING
Courtesy Arizona Republic

DON'T GET SICK

JACK JURDEN
Courtesy Wilmington Evening Journal–News

DANA SUMMERS
Courtesy Journal Herald (Ohio)

The IRS is fed up with bad press. Commissioner Egger plans some action.

— *Wall Street Journal item*

"And perhaps if I changed my brand of after-shave . . ."

HUGH HAYNIE
Courtesy Louisville Courier-Journal

154

CORKY
Courtesy Honolulu Star–Bulletin

"Terrorism—the beast of our times"

LA BESTIA DE NUESTRO TIEMPO

ANGEL ZAMARRIPAL
Mexico

Evolution of man as peacemaker

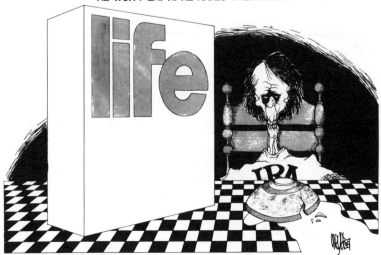

"HE WON'T EAT IT. HE HATES EVERYTHING."

TOM MEYER
Courtesy San Francisco Chronicle

"PEOPLE OUGHT TO BE AS SMART AS A HOG"– SECRETARY JOHN R. BLOCK

ART WOOD
Courtesy AFBF (Md.)

DANI AGUILA
Courtesy Filipino Reporter

CHUCK BROOKS
Courtesy Birmingham News

Past Award Winners

PULITZER PRIZE EDITORIAL CARTOON

1922—Rollin Kirby, New York World
1924—J. N. Darling, New York Herald Tribune
1925—Rollin Kirby, New York World
1926—D. R. Fitzpatrick, St. Louis Post-Dispatch
1927—Nelson Harding, Brooklyn Eagle
1928—Nelson Harding, Brooklyn Eagle
1929—Rollin Kirby, New York World
1930—Charles Macauley, Brooklyn Eagle
1931—Edmund Duffy, Baltimore Sun
1932—John T. McCutcheon, Chicago Tribune
1933—H. M. Talburt, Washington Daily News
1934—Edmund Duffy, Baltimore Sun
1935—Ross A. Lewis, Milwaukee Journal
1937—C. D. Batchelor, New York Daily News
1938—Vaughn Shoemaker, Chicago Daily News
1939—Charles G. Werner, Daily Oklahoman
1940—Edmund Duffy, Baltimore Sun
1941—Jacob Burck, Chicago Times
1942—Herbert L. Block, Newspaper Enterprise Association
1943—Jay N. Darling, New York Herald Tribune
1944—Clifford K. Berryman, Washington Star
1945—Bill Mauldin, United Feature Syndicate
1946—Bruce Russell, Los Angeles Times
1947—Vaughn Shoemaker, Chicago Daily News
1948—Reuben L. (Rube) Goldberg, New York Sun
1949—Lute Pease, Newark Evening News
1950—James T. Berryman, Washington Star
1951—Reginald W. Manning, Arizona Republic
1952—Fred L. Packer, New York Mirror
1953—Edward D. Kuekes, Cleveland Plain Dealer
1954—Herbert L. Block, Washington Post
1955—Daniel R. Fitzpatrick, St. Louis Post-Dispatch
1956—Robert York, Louisville Times
1957—Tom Little, Nashville Tennessean
1958—Bruce M. Shanks, Buffalo Evening News
1959—Bill Mauldin, St. Louis Post-Dispatch
1961—Carey Orr, Chicago Tribune
1962—Edmund S. Valtman, Hartford Times
1963—Frank Miller, Des Moines Register
1964—Paul Conrad, Denver Post
1966—Don Wright, Miami News
1967—Patrick B. Oliphant, Denver Post
1968—Eugene Gray Payne, Charlotte Observer
1969—John Fischetti, Chicago Daily News
1970—Thomas F. Darcy, Newsday
1971—Paul Conrad, Los Angeles Times
1972—Jeffrey K. MacNelly, Richmond News Leader
1974—Paul Szep, Boston Globe
1975—Garry Trudeau, Universal Press Syndicate
1976—Tony Auth, Philadelphia Enquirer
1977—Paul Szep, Boston Globe
1978—Jeff MacNelly, Richmond News Leader
1979—Herbert Block, Washington Post
1980—Don Wright, Miami News
1981—Mike Peters, Dayton Daily News

NOTE: Pulitzer Prize Award was not given 1923, 1936, 1960, 1965, and 1973.

SIGMA DELTA CHI AWARD EDITORIAL CARTOON

1942—Jacob Burck, Chicago Times
1943—Charles Werner, Chicago Sun
1944—Henry Barrow, Associated Press
1945—Reuben L. Goldberg, New York Sun
1946—Dorman H. Smith, Newspaper Enterprise Association
1947—Bruce Russell, Los Angeles Times
1948—Herbert Block, Washington Post
1949—Herbert Block, Washington Post
1950—Bruce Russell, Los Angeles Times
1951—Herbert Block, Washington Post, and
        Bruce Russell, Los Angeles Times
1952—Cecil Jensen, Chicago Daily News
1953—John Fischetti, Newspaper Enterprise Association
1954—Calvin Alley, Memphis Commercial Appeal
1955—John Fischetti, Newspaper Enterprise Association
1956—Herbert Block, Washington Post
1957—Scott Long, Minneapolis Tribune
1958—Clifford H. Baldowski, Atlanta Constitution
1959—Charles G. Brooks, Birmingham News
1960—Dan Dowling, New York Herald-Tribune
1961—Frank Interlandi, Des Moines Register
1962—Paul Conrad, Denver Post
1963—William Mauldin, Chicago Sun-Times
1964—Charles Bissell, Nashville Tennessean
1965—Roy Justus, Minneapolis Star
1966—Patrick Oliphant, Denver Post
1967—Eugene Payne, Charlotte Observer
1968—Paul Conrad, Los Angeles Times
1969—William Mauldin, Chicago Sun-Times
1970—Paul Conrad, Los Angeles Times
1971—Hugh Haynie, Louisville Courier-Journal
1972—William Mauldin, Chicago Sun-Times
1973—Paul Szep, Boston Globe
1974—Mike Peters, Dayton Daily News
1975—Tony Auth, Philadelphia Enquirer
1976—Paul Szep, Boston Globe
1977—Don Wright, Miami News
1978—Jim Borgman, Cincinnati Enquirer
1979—John P. Trever, Albuquerque Journal
1980—Paul Conrad, Los Angeles Times

NATIONAL HEADLINERS CLUB AWARD EDITORIAL CARTOON

1938—C. D. Batchelor, New York Daily News
1939—John Knott, Dallas News
1940—Herbert Block, Newspaper Enterprise Association
1941—Charles H. Sykes, Philadelphia Evening Ledger
1942—Jerry Doyle, Philadelphia Record
1943—Vaughn Shoemaker, Chicago Daily News
1944—Roy Justus, Sioux City Journal
1945—F. O. Alexander, Philadelphia Bulletin
1946—Hank Barrow, Associated Press
1947—Cy Hungerford, Pittsburgh Post-Gazette
1948—Tom Little, Nashville Tennessean
1949—Bruce Russell, Los Angeles Times
1950—Dorman Smith, Newspaper Enterprise Association
1951—C. G. Werner, Indianapolis Star
1952—John Fischetti, Newspaper Enterprise Association
1953—James T. Berryman and Gib Crockett, Washington Star
1954—Scott Long, Minneapolis Tribune
1955—Leo Thiele, Los Angeles Mirror-News
1956—John Milt Morris, Associated Press
1957—Frank Miller, Des Moines Register
1958—Burris Jenkins, Jr., New York Journal-American
1959—Karl Hubenthal, Los Angeles Examiner
1960—Don Hesse, St. Louis Globe-Democrat
1961—L. D. Warren, Cincinnati Enquirer
1962—Franklin Morse, Los Angeles Mirror
1963—Charles Bissell, Nashville Tennessean
1964—Lou Grant, Oakland Tribune
1965—Merle R. Tingley, London (Ont.) Free Press
1966—Hugh Haynie, Louisville Courier-Journal
1967—Jim Berry, Newspaper Enterprise Association
1968—Warren King, New York News
1969—Larry Barton, Toledo Blade
1970—Bill Crawford, Newspaper Enterprise Association
1971—Ray Osrin, Cleveland Plain Dealer
1972—Jacob Burck, Chicago Sun-Times
1973—Ranan Lurie, New York Times
1974—Tom Darcy, Newsday
1975—Bill Sanders, Milwaukee Journal
1976—No award given
1977—Paul Szep, Boston Globe
1978—Dwane Powell, Raleigh News and Observer
1979—Pat Oliphant, Washington Star
1980—Don Wright, Miami News
1981—Bill Garner, Memphis Commercial Appeal

NATIONAL NEWSPAPER AWARD/CANADA EDITORIAL CARTOON

1949—Jack Boothe, Toronto Globe and Mail
1950—James G. Reidford, Montreal Star
1951—Len Norris, Vancouver Sun
1952—Robert La Palme, Le Devoir, Montreal
1953—Robert W. Chambers, Halifax Chronicle-Herald
1954—John Collins, Montreal Gazette
1955—Merle R. Tingley, London Free Press
1956—James G. Reidford, Toronto Globe and Mail
1957—James G. Reidford, Toronto Globe and Mail
1958—Raoul Hunter, Le Soleil, Quebec
1959—Duncan Macpherson, Toronto Star
1960—Duncan Macpherson, Toronto Star
1961—Ed McNally, Montreal Star
1962—Duncan Macpherson, Toronto Star
1963—Jan Kamienski, Winnipeg Tribune
1964—Ed McNally, Montreal Star
1965—Duncan Macpherson, Toronto Star
1966—Robert W. Chambers, Halifax Chronicle-Herald
1967—Raoul Hunter, Le Soleil, Quebec
1968—Roy Peterson, Vancouver Sun
1969—Edward Uluschak, Edmonton Journal
1970—Duncan Macpherson, Toronto Daily Star
1971—Yardley Jones, Toronto Sun
1972—Duncan Macpherson, Toronto Star
1973—John Collins, Montreal Gazette
1974—Blaine, Hamilton Spectator
1975—Roy Peterson, Vancouver Sun
1976—Andy Donato, Toronto Sun
1977—Terry Mosher, Montreal Gazette
1978—Terry Mosher, Montreal Gazette
1979—Edd Uluschak, Edmonton Journal
1980—Vic Roschkov, Toronto Star

OVERSEAS PRESS CLUB AWARD EDITORIAL CARTOON

1970—Tom Darcy, Newsday
1971—Don Wright, Miami News
1972—Tom Darcy, Newsday
1973—Warren King, New York Daily News
1974—Tony Auth, Philadelphia Inquirer
1975—Tony Auth, Philadelphia Inquirer
1976—Warren King, New York Daily News
1977—Ed Fischer, Omaha World-Herald
1978—Jim Morin, Miami Herald
1979—Don Wright, Miami News
1980—Paul Conrad, Los Angeles Times

Index

INDEX